EA
(Evangelical A

CW01502479

THE FIRST 40 YEARS
(1938 – 1978)

John Philip Medcraft

John Philip Medcraft

EAB
(Evangelical Action Brazil)

THE FIRST 40 YEARS
(1938 – 1978)

November 2012

In memory of the dedicated service of founder pioneer EAB missionaries Albert Mundy and Frank Dyer.

"To God be the glory – great things He has done".

Contents

Preface

This book is not an exercise in Mission marketing, but an honest upfront account of the first 40 years of EAB when we got it right and when we got it wrong. It is a mark of honour to dedicated missionaries who gave their best for Jesus in north-east Brazil

EAB's first 40 years covered a period of great change and turmoil. Within a year of the Mission's founding the Second World War erupted. Later in the period there was the 1964 Coup d'état in Brazil which ushered in 20 years under a military regime.

Travel to Brazil in the early years by ship changed to planes. Telegrams were substituted by telephones and radios were joined by black and white TVs. Earth tracks were partially substituted by tarmac roads as the period progressed and vehicles began to replace horses and mules for travel. Electricity was initially generated locally in Patos, but eventually was integrated to the national grid. Water started to be piped to people's houses rather than being carried by donkeys or carts, though the latter still continues in the interior of Paraíba State to this day. Cesspits linked to holes in the ground were progress from random defecation and still today only 7% of the homes in Patos are linked to the sewage treatment plant.

In the religious sphere Catholicism was the dominant force and EAB faced strong opposition to its preaching the Biblical Gospel of Jesus Christ, often violent and always insulting our folk as being part of a dangerous sect. EAB had been directed by God to plant evangelical churches in the poorest, driest and most spiritually barren region of Brazil. We pay homage to those missionaries and national workers who tirelessly served God in an area few wanted to live or work in and we praise God for their lives and ministries.

John Philip Medcraft
Patos, Paraíba
North-east Brazil
15th November 2012 (43rd wedding anniversary)

1. Nomansland

Evangelical Action (Brazil), known for short as EAB, started its existence in 1938 as The Gospel to Brazil Faith Mission, or just GTB. It was born in a period of church history when faith missions sprouted profusely from a fresh wave of evangelical fervour. There was also a special interest in Brazil amongst evangelicals who felt the impact of the 1910 World Missionary Conference, held in Edinburgh, which had come to the unbelievable conclusion that Latin America did not really need missionaries because the Roman Catholic Church was already there!

The house where Albert Mundy was born in East Tytherley

The founder of EAB was Albert Edward Mundy, born on 17th July 1904 at East Tytherley, Hampshire, which today is the smallest village in the River Test Valley. It is situated, as the crow flies, about half way between Winchester and Salisbury, being 16 miles from Southampton.

Albert Mundy's family was poor, honest and working class. His father was a shepherd. He had several brothers and sisters, and whilst he was still a child the family moved to Nomansland in the New Forest. In his teens Albert became a farm worker on the Lyburn Estate there.

On 27th February 1923, at the age of 18, he heard the Gospel preached at a Methodist Chapel at Nomansland, through the ministry of a woman called Greta. Albert Mundy, and some of his mates, had been making a nuisance of themselves at the church and ended up getting locked out. Boys will be boys, and they decided to climb up on an outer wall and peer through the window to continue hearing Ms. Greta. However Albert started feeling that she was preaching and pointing directly at him; God dealt with him, and he was soundly converted.

Some time later Albert met Daisy Weeks, from the Isle of Wight, who was working at Bramshaw Vicarage. They married on 4th June 1927 at Bramshaw and lived in a little bungalow in School Road, Nomansland.

In 1930 and 1931 Albert Mundy increasingly felt God calling him to Christian ministry, and it appears that a book about Ernest George Fenton Hall, a young missionary who lost his life serving God in Brazil, was significant in pointing Albert in that direction for missionary service. Albert's son, Graham, told me that his father felt strongly on his heart to reach Brazilian Indians, so this would certainly tie up with the Fenton Hall influence, because he worked amongst the Indians in the Amazon region and his journals were published by WEC in 1925. This theory is corroborated by a letter and report received by EAB in 1972 from Sidney A. Dance of Southampton. His wife had collected a series of jottings about the call and ministry of Albert Mundy, and he forwarded them to our office. The Dances had been early supporters of EAB and in Mrs. Dance's jottings she notes that Albert read Fenton Hall's book prior to feeling God's call to Brazil.

Thus Albert said that it was in 1931 that God gave him a verse of Scripture, as a promise for the years ahead, in a version of

Proverbs 4:12 which says, "As thou goest, step by step, so the way shall open up before thee". This text was later to become EAB's motto for many years.

Although it was not till 1938 that Albert and Daisy Mundy left for missionary work in Brazil, all through the period leading up to this Albert was confident of God's guidance into Christian ministry in Brazil. One step at a time he felt God was opening up the way for his life. Thus Albert and Daisy gained experience and were prepared by God for the mission field over a seven year period. Albert was always enthusiastic to tell others about Jesus and preached a lot in the local chapels.

It was at this time that Albert and Daisy Mundy joined the Gospel Hall in Canada Road, West Wellow. It is a small church but a faithful church, having supported EAB right from the beginning to the present day. At West Wellow Albert formed a group of young men known as Gospel trekkers, and for a fortnight annually (during five years), this group used to take off to unknown destinations; cycling with the Gospel, distributing Gospel tracts and Bible portions and preaching in the towns and villages as they went. The first year took them to Weston-Super-Mare, and the following years to Exeter, Birmingham and Nottingham. On the fifth year they evangelized the Isle of White on foot! Albert Mundy was accompanied on these treks by Arthur Snelgrove, Mr. Bannister, Stanley Dibden and Elgie Bergersen, and the latter two were active as 'EAB supporters' right from the start.

All through the 1930s Albert Mundy was increasingly feeling God's call on his life to Brazil, but it was his wife, Daisy, who dragged her feet. In her written testimony Daisy admits that for years she "was stubborn and wouldn't give in". However at the beginning of 1938 two dramatic incidents changed everything, for Albert suffered two bad accidents in five weeks and God spoke to Daisy through these. First of all Albert had an accident with an electric saw at Lyburn Farm, which badly injured his arm. Then a few weeks later he was nearly killed when a horse he was holding reared in fright, caused by a passing bus near Bramshaw church, and crashed down on Albert giving him terrible head injuries.

Albert remained unconscious for many days. *"I felt increasingly guilty,"* Daisy admits in her testimony, *"and I knew that God was using those accidents to speak to me because of my disobedience. One night the doctor said there was no hope for my husband so I told God that if He gave me back my husband I would go where He wanted me to go. From that day on Bert began to make progress and his recovery was then really quick."* God healed Albert Mundy. It was the changing point in that couple's lives before God, and the start of Evangelical Action (Brazil).

Once recovered, Albert Mundy began to make definitive preparations to leave the UK for Brazil and made various applications to UK Missionary Societies, *"but was accepted by none,"* he remarked in an early letter.

So it was that E. Bergersen informs us, in early EAB publications, that he took part in the production of the first Mission prayer letter with Albert Mundy in April 1938. Unfortunately this letter has been lost, but Mr. Bergersen says that it had the title "The Gospel to Brazil" and it is clear that the Mundys intended to leave for Brazil on 28th May.

The title "The Gospel to Brazil" was in keeping with names used in those days by evangelical missions. Sarah Kalley, widow of the great Congregational pioneer in Brazil, Robert Kalley, called the mission she created in 1892 "Help for Brazil". This was later to become EUSA (Evangelical Union of South America) and today is known as Latin Link. So too, EAB commenced as "The Gospel to Brazil", 4 months later became "The Gospel to Brazil Faith Mission" (GTB), and today has become Evangelical Action (Brazil) or EAB. Such changes are natural progressions which embrace cultural, linguistic and religious changes over a period of time.

Albert and Daisy Mundy were not able to leave for Brazil on 28th May 1938 because they could not obtain their visas in time. This they made clear in their second prayer newsletter of August that year which EAB archives do contain. The letter shows the simple way in which EAB commenced its existence. For it was only as the

14

Brazilian authorities confronted Albert Mundy about how he would be financially supported, that he realized the need to have a secretary and treasurer in the UK; so Pastor Winston Shearing, (then of Verwood in Dorset), was *"appointed"* to both roles. Thus 1938 was a dramatic year in the life of Albert Mundy. At its beginning he was nearly killed, but on 13th April he and his wife had obtained a dual passport from the Foreign Office in London, and on 2nd August they received their visa to enter Brazil at Pernambuco State, north-eastern Brazil. So the Mundys announced the booking of their passages to Brazil for 20th August 1938 on the HMS Almanzora, *"going aboard at 11 o'clock"*.

Their fares to Brazil were paid by a lady called Miss Clark, whom the Mundys had not met until the day of their departure. She had heard of them and sent them a cheque from where she lived at Tunbridge Wells, but we do not know how she knew them.

2. Almanzora

Source: novomilenio.inf.br

HMS Almanzora

On the day the Mundys sailed to Brazil a large crowd of supporters, led by Pastor Winston Shearing, gathered at the Southampton docks to bid them farewell. Amongst the crowd of about 60 present we know that the following were there: William Frank Mundy (Albert's father), Mary Mundy (Albert's mother), Dorothy Mundy (sister), John Dibden (Dorothy's 'young man' who she later married), Ron Mundy (brother), Frederick Shearing and his sons Winston and Lloyd; Frank Hurst, Raymond Hurst, Phyllis Hurst, Brenda Hurst; Frank Dyer, Jack Dyer, Gwen Dyer, Bertha Dyer, Fred and Amy Snelgrove, Ena Snelgrove, Esme Snelgrove, Dorothy Bannister (Esme's aunt), Bernard Snelgrove, Vera Snelgrove, Mary and Norman Read (Vera's relatives from London); Ernie and John Dawkins, Elgernon (Elgie) and Elsie Bergersen, Arthur King (Nomansland), Ada Clewer, Edna Welstead and Miss Clarke (who paid the missionaries fares to Brazil). Most of the ladies wore hats and most of the men and boys wore caps, whilst some wore Trilby hats. They sang hymns (one of the hymns we know they sang was *"I know the Lord will make a way for me"*), they prayed, they wept, and they waved as the HMS

Almanzora pulled away past the Isle of Wight in the direction of the equator.

EAB's pioneer missionaries being bid farewell

HMS Almanzora was a 16,000 ton cargo and passenger ship used by the Royal Mail, which had been built in Northern Ireland and launched in 1914. In World War I it was transformed into an armed Cruiser, and in World War II it became a troop carrier. Now it was a carrier of the soldiers of Christ. Between wars, the Almanzora could carry 400 first class passengers, 230 second class and 760 third class. EAB's founders were only able to afford the latter category which clearly was not much fun.

Once the ship set sail, Albert Mundy was quick to get to his typewriter and was typing a letter to the Hurst family at West Wellow by 3.30pm. *"I must say how much we were moved by the wonderful send off...the whole Ship saw the testimony and we have already heard remarks regarding it... we have had a nice talk to an Indian and trust we may lead him to Christ before we reach Lisbon...ever in the bonds of Calvary...Bert & Daisy."*

The Mundys entered Brazil at the north-east port of Recife on 2nd September 1938. The Brazilian Maritime and Air Police stamped their joint passport on this day. Albert already had a receding hairline above his blue eyes, at his age then of 34, but his passport photo shows he still had plenty of bushy light brown hair above that. Neither Albert nor his wife were tall and were both registered as 5 ft. 2 inches in height. They stayed with a Swedish missionary couple by the name of Carson, and soon Albert was writing to the Hurst family again in England. *"Praise God for safe arrival here... we had a really good voyage. I was only sick for about half an hour. It soon passed off and we were able to enjoy the journey. When the heat was getting unbearable the Lord caused the wind to become strong and the waves beat up above our cabin porthole and so kept the place cool as we were unable to keep the cabin door open because the smell of the people was awful...The Lord has undertaken when we reached Pernambuco and we had nothing to pay on going through customs... now we look forward to speaking the language".* Albert went on to talk about the bureaucratic red tape involved in getting themselves established in the country, including having their finger prints taken 13 times each, but remarked that he would not want to be anywhere else.

On 12th December 1938, as Christmas approached, the tone of a new letter is a little bit low as both missionaries were suffering with boils, and receiving lots of hassle from the authorities, in their on-going saga to be legally registered as foreign citizens in Brazil on a permanent basis, and had to have vaccinations and medical examinations. Nevertheless Albert was *"still shouting victory"* because he had just preached his first message in Brazil, through an American interpreter at a Swedish Pentecostal Church, when five accepted the Lord as Saviour. Two days after Christmas he wrote again, thrilled at having received a parcel of apples and marrow jam from England which was *"the best I have ever tasted"!* The boils had now cleared up and they were feeling more positive, but frustrated still at not being able to speak Portuguese.

19

How exactly the Mundys met the Swedish missionaries, the Carlsons, we do not exactly know. Jottings by Daisy Mundy tell us that *"the first person to meet us was an ex-missionary from England who was living with the Carlsons who were Swedish missionaries and they invited us to stay at their orphanage until we got the language. We got on very well with Mr. Carlson who helped us a lot"*. What is not clear from Mrs. Mundy's account, is whether they met this ex-missionary from England on the ship or when they arrived in Brazil. However the Carson family was an important anchor family for the start of EAB, and the Carlsons were still friends with EAB missionaries in the 1970s, because I was taken to their house for a meal the first evening I arrived in Brazil in 1972.

Prayer letter number No. 4 for January 1939 still described their on-going battle with the authorities for permanent residence in Brazil, and their documents had now been sent to Rio de Janeiro for verification. In a personal letter near the end of the month, the Mundys are clearly getting more into the swing of Brazilian life at Beberibe, Recife; seeing snakes and monkeys and mixing more with the people. Albert remarks, *"The people here are many of them very black, but the real Brazilian is a dark brown, or reddish colour, but very kind and nice when you get to know them. Sunday we had our first meal in a Brazilian home...a hut made of sticks and mud and covered with a long grass. They don't separate the food like us but put it in a heap and mix it all together... beans, sweet potatoes, shou-shou like small marrow, chicken, rice, farinha, maize meal... fish too"*. At the end Albert comments that they are progressing with the language so people had better watch out when they visit England, as we *"will be able to say just what we like about you"*!

Albert Mundy's first journey to the interior was reported in the Mission's 5th Prayer Letter for February and March 1939 because he had travelled on a train to Jaboatão. Mundy remarks that the train was more like *"our cattle trucks"* but they made it safely to the service, where again he preached through an interpreter. Jaboatão today is very much part of the massive city of Recife, but clearly then it was *"interior"*. Then on 5th February 1939 Mundy ventured on a *"long journey to Florença dos Leões"* travelling *"by motor"* through very *"rough and lonely country, forests and mountains. It was a very rough track. We received much shaking"*. He however was thrilled to see many gathering to hear the Gospel at their destination.

Albert Mundy's travels continued to be reported in EAB's Prayer letter No. 6 of May 1939, as he continued to travel with his Swedish missionary friends to Pau D'alho and as far as Caruaru, some 90 miles, to preach the Gospel. He replies in a personal letter to Phyllis Hurst on May Day that she had arrived late with the news of Eddie Irish's marriage, as he had already received a piece of wedding cake and found it very good! He complained however because she had sent him a copy of the News of the World newspaper; of which he did not approve. Constantly in good spirits, Albert lamented the death of Phyllis's cat which he had learnt of, and ended the letter saying that his wife sent her love and *"I hope it won't drop out on the way"*!

EAB's first anniversary in August 1939 was celebrated with the missionaries still in Recife, but feeling definite direction from God to move where people had not yet heard the Gospel. Albert Mundy also complained about the June St. John's Festival he had experienced for the first time, with its bonfires and fireworks in honour of the saint describing it as *"darkness of the worst kind"*. This traditional festival throughout north-eastern Brazil is darker than ever today as the all-night parties, which in some places go on for the whole month of June; involve drugs, heavy drinking, promiscuity, and noise at levels Pastor Mundy would not have dreamed possible. Today Patos, EAB's headquarters, is the centre of distribution of the drug "crack" for the whole of north-east Brazil. It is indeed "darkness of the worst kind".

However as EAB was celebrating its first anniversary, and its first missionary couple was adapting well to Brazil and getting to grips with the Portuguese language, war clouds were gathering fast in Europe, and in September 1939 Germany invaded Poland so France, Great Britain and the Commonwealth declared war on Germany. The Second World War had begun, and throughout the war years we are deprived of the letters that flowed between Phyllis Hurst and the EAB missionaries in Brazil. This unfortunately limits our options of research during this period. Nevertheless the official EAB Newsletters were maintained so the story of the Mission can still be followed.

3. World War II

The outbreak of war immediately made life complicated for EAB in many ways. There was an initial breakdown in communication between Brazil and the UK, and after Prayer Letter 7, and its references to the first year of the Mission and the first anniversary, it took till January 1940 to produce the next letter and this was written by the *"Honorary General Secretary: Pastor W. Shearing, 'Ferndale', Ringwood Road, Verwood, Dorset"*, and not by the Mundys. Thus Pastor Shearing wrote: *"I am writing as our Brother, Mr. Mundy, has requested... at present it is very difficult to communicate with him; the only way is by Air Mail...With everything so dark around us, we as Children of Light, need to be more prayerful... it has been a time of severe testing"*.

Pastor Shearing then went on to tell of the difficulties EAB was having in sending financial support to the missionaries, and the different ways they had tried. He also said that EAB prayer meetings had commenced at the "village of Canada" which presumably refers to Canada Road, West Wellow, and at Fawley. In fact in the EAB archives we have an account by E. Bergersen as follows:

"The Gospel to Brazil Faith Mission...The Fawley Friends...The first prayer meeting for the GTB as held at the new church at Hardley, the first Tuesday of the month 6th February 1940...Meeting started at 7.45pm...as I entered they were singing 'The need of the world is Jesus'. The leader was Frank Dyer (Local Sec). The first hymn, Redemption Songs 634 'Far away in heathen darkness dwelling'. Then we turned to heaven as our leader led in prayer...we thought of the great need of Brazil sixty times the size of Great Britain, forty million human souls. Prayer was interposed with special requests". The service ended after 9pm and the next meeting was fixed for March 5th 1940.

Surely EAB's UK supporters were right to increase prayer support because things were not easy for the Mundy's in Brazil. Their Prayer Letter No. 9 of March 1940 tells of how the missionaries now felt cut off as they "hadn't heard from anyone for months". They also informed supporters that they had now left Recife and were living in the interior of the State of Pernambuco, as from 16th March 1940, but they do not specify where that was. It was Garanhuns, 142 miles from Recife; because we know they were living there in May 1940 and were shocked by the high levels of illiteracy which made it impossible to work with Gospel tracts.

The town of Garanhuns has a much cooler climate than Recife so that would have been enjoyed by the Mundys. They appear to have come here through contacts with an American missionary friend, but when they arrived they discovered he had left. It must be remembered that the EAB missionaries were still in the process of learning Portuguese, and becoming more accustomed to Brazilian culture and climate, so Garanhuns was a clear step to the needy interior but far from what they had on their hearts. Albert and Daisy Mundy were by now feeling confident enough to step out alone to unevangelized towns and villages further in the interior, and this was certainly not the case in Garanhuns. For evangelical Presbyterians had been well established in Garanhuns since the very beginning of the 20th century and founded an excellent school there, *"Colégio 15 de Novembro"*, in 1908. Garanhuns was therefore a helpful stepping stone away from the coast, but was not for EAB in those days.

Thus in 1940 the Mundys came to be based at Garanhuns, but travelled around preaching in different places and seeking the direction of God as to where exactly they should establish a base; but this they felt needed to be in an area of great spiritual and physical need where there was no established evangelical ministry. Albert Mundy thought about going south to the State of Alagoas, and visited Crato, further north in the state of Ceará. However at no point does he seem to be considering the state of Paraíba where in fact he ended up. In November 1940 Albert writes:

"I had a desire to go south, but could not be clear about the matter. But prayer was made to God for almost a week".

Finally Albert and Daisy Mundy felt it was time to step out in faith the next day, 7th November 1940, and come what may they would get on whatever vehicle turned up in Garanhuns that day and take its destination as the will of God. They packed their trunks, waited and prayed. The following day a lorry laden high with cotton pulled into town and Albert asked the driver where he was going? *"Flores"*, was the answer. *"We'll go with you"*, Albert replied, and they loaded up their earthly possessions amongst the cotton and soon were on their way. They were heading north-west near to the border with the State of Paraíba, and they arrived in Flores the same day.

The missionaries found somewhere to sleep for the night in Flores, and in the morning of 8th November they travelled the 12 miles across the Paraíba border to Princesa Isabel. EAB had come to stay!

4. EAB's First Headquarters

8th November 1940 was an historical day for the Mission because it was the start of phase two of the Mundys' ministry in Brazil; It was the start of work in the State of Paraíba where EAB has been based ever since, and Princesa Isabel was to be the town in which EAB built its first church in 1943. Between 1940 and 1948 Princesa Isabel was to be the headquarters of EAB before it moved to Patos, where it is to this day.

It is amazing how God works, and I cannot be sure if Brother Mundy knew that a EUSA (Latin Link) missionary and colporteur, called Frederick C. Glass, had visited Princesa Isabel (at the time just known as Princesa), some 10 years earlier selling Bibles. F. C. Glass's grandson, Philip Glass, is a friend of mine, and a fine Christian, who today is living in Rio de Janeiro where he runs an excellent charity for the blind. I have F. C. Glass's book *'Through Brazilian Junglelands with the Book'* in which he tells of his colporteur work in Princesa Isabel, Flores and Tavares (around 1930) which he visited whilst based at Garanhuns. The similarities in the locations involved lead me to speculate that Albert Mundy either had met Frederick Glass in the UK or Brazil, or perhaps read his journals and books, but of this I cannot be sure.

Frederick Glass, according to his book sold Bibles in the Princesa area between May 1928 and April 1931; but I presume we can be sure it was prior to 1930 as there was a very bloody uprising in Princesa in 1930, involving a stand off and battle between the local and state authorities of the Governor, João Pessoa, which Glass surely would have mentioned had he been there after this infamous incident.

F. C. Glass first went to Tavares where EAB today has two churches, one in the town and one in a rural area. He then travelled the 16 miles to Princesa in his Ford car because a local State Deputy *"was anxious we should visit his city, where the Gospel had never been preached"*. Today EAB has a thriving church in the town and a Bible College, plus a church in the rural area at

Cedro, and other daughter churches in the region. On Glass's visit he sold a number of Bibles and Testaments. The seed was sown. One plants, another waters, *"but God gives the increase"!* (I Corinthians 3:6) Today EAB has churches in the region.

Looking back over the spread of the Gospel in that part of Paraíba, one cannot but notice the strategic planning of the sovereign Lord. God is like a mighty chess player who never loses a game, but knows exactly when to move an appropriate piece into position. It is humbling and glorious to be part of God's magnificent strategy to save the lost.

Thus Albert Mundy was writing in November 1940, in Newsletter No.15, that he had received a hostile reception from the local Roman Catholic priest and his followers upon arriving at Princesa. He wrote:

"The boast of the priest was: 'I have confidence in our Lady that the Gospel shall never enter Princesa'. But praise God it has! The day I arrived there I heard that there was one Christian who was living there and I sought her out. To my amazement she said as I approached her, 'Are you the Pastor we have been waiting for? We have been praying for a year'! We arranged a meeting for that same night when crowds gathered to hear for the first time in their lives the simple Gospel message".

For days after this Albert Mundy preached every night in Princesa, gathering large numbers to hear. The priest had already cursed the missionaries, and announced that it was a deadly sin to listen to them or even see them! This did much to arouse the people against them, and in the service one night a man arrived with an 18-inch knife and some rope announcing that the knife was to kill the goat, (i.e. a protestant who is not a sheep), and the rope was to tie up the *cabras,* (i.e. she goats, which must have referred to Daisy and the other Christian lady in town). However Albert was preaching with armed policemen present, so the incident just remained verbal and not physical. Three men were arrested during the week's meetings for causing disturbances, but another lady came to Christ. At the time, Albert Mundy reported that he was being given police

28

protection still for every service he held. All this police protection was possible because a Christian Chief of Police was moved into Princesa one month before the Mundys' arrival!

Albert Mundy also commented that the priest started spreading lies round town that Albert was paying people to become Christians. One night Albert was attacked by stoning from a mob, but managed to escape unhurt. He also commented in the newsletter that where he was, he was cut off from outside news, and had no idea how the war was going. In Letter N° 16 Albert Mundy said they had not received money for months and couldn't even rent a house without it, but were dependent on a loaned room in someone's house.

5. EAB Home Organization

In 1941 EAB firmly took on more shape as an organized Mission when on 18th January the first Committee or Mission Board was formed in the UK, and held its inaugural meeting. Up till this point things had been done informally by different brethren with Pastor Shearing coordinating, but now a Board was formed. Eddie Irish was the Committee Chairman, Pastor Winston Shearing continued–as from the beginning–as the Secretary, E. Bergersen became the Treasurer, and the other members were Frank Dyer and Stanley Dibden.

Special EAB services were announced for the Easter Monday afternoon and evening at Bethel Chapel, Verwood, and the third EAB anniversary service was announced for 20th August at West Wellow. Continued EAB prayer meetings were confirmed at West Wellow on the third Thursday of every month, and at Hardley Green on the first Tuesday in each month. Thus EAB was growing in structure and this structure was firmly built on prayer.

The Committee announced also in 1941 that as the war meant only airmail letters could be sent to Brazil, it would gather everyone's letters on lightweight paper in the first week of each month, to economize by sending them together. Clearly airmail was an expensive option in those days, but the committee realized how important it was to maintain contact with their missionaries and show they had not been forgotten. A hand written addendum to Prayer Letter N° 16 praised God because news had just arrived that £20 had reached Mr. Mundy.

6. Roots and Fruits

By mid 1941 the ministry of Albert and Daisy Mundy at Princesa Isabel was putting down roots despite constant threats, intimidation and opposition, and they were preparing five new converts for baptism. In October of that year they were asking prayer concerning their desire to reach Flores and Tavares. However the priest in Flores had blocked the rental of a small house for meetings by threatening the owner if she rented it to Protestants; and Friar Damião, an infamous radical anti-Protestant, had been to Flores to whip up opposition. Despite this, Albert already speaks of Joaquim Faustino as having been appointed as local leader of the work there, and of a few faithful going to the meetings.

One useful weapon which Daisy Mundy had in those days of religious prejudice and persecution was her harp. The fact that she played the harp and a mandolin probably explains the genetic source of her son Graham's great musical ability. The fact is that the soothing sound of the harp broke down barriers. People were fascinated and wanted to watch and listen, and they would leave a copy of a Gospel with the family at the end. One day, on the bumpy road back to Princesa from evangelizing at Flores, the harp fell off the back of the lorry they were travelling in and nobody noticed. They had given it up for lost when the next day one of the converts at Flores turned up with it. The casing was smashed, but the harp survived and would need new strings from England; this was not easy in the war. Nevertheless, with the Lord's help, the UK Committee managed to get them to Brazil and the harp played on.

In May 1942 Daisy writes about the conversion of a murderer, José Paulino, in the Princesa Isabel jail upon hearing her husband preach the Gospel, and that now he had been released and was strong in the Lord. Others had come to Christ at Princesa Isabel by then, though some had gone away to find work in view of the drought, which is a constant problem in the semi-arid region of north-eastern Brazil to this day. In Prayer Letter 21 Mrs. Mundy reports the purchase of land in Princesa Isabel, by faith, to build the first EAB church! Already Albert Mundy and José Paulino were making the doors and windows, and others from the little church were bringing bricks to the site ready to start construction. Daisy mentions how hard the work is with all the wood needing to be sawn by hand from trees, but they were clearly excited about having a church to house the *"16 converts and many children at Princesa... and it seems to be the ones who were most opposed to us when we got here who are getting converted first! Nothing is too hard for the Lord"*.

Finally on 11th August 1942, almost 4 years after their arrival in Brazil, Albert and Daisy Mundy received their official authorization to stay permanently in the country, and they were overjoyed. I have before me Albert Mundy's identity card which is more like an identity passport. Inside the document the different addresses the Mundy's lived at are recorded. They were registered at João Pessoa Avenue in "Princesa" in 1942 but on 26th May 1948 they moved to Espinharas Street in Patos. The last address registered is Padre Anchieta Street, 544, in Patos, which is where his late son Graham's widow lives to this day. Bert Mundy was registered as foreigner number 61.942 and the son of William Frank Mundy and Mary Mundy. Brother Mundy refers to finally obtaining these permanent documents as *"one of the greatest victories for the future of the Mission and the progress of the work here"*. At this time the Mundys started to ask for prayer for a "native worker" to be raised up to work with them, and for the appropriate support to be found for this. Albert suggests that EAB consult Peniel Chapel, my home church, about the costs involved as "they will have more information and have more experience". Clearly the work was expanding and the missionaries needed help to cope. In fact in late 1942 Albert reports having been ministering in Campina Grande, so he was indeed spreading his wings.

Back in the UK a change had to be made in the EAB Committee, as Frank Dyer received his call up to join the war effort in the British army in the latter part of 1942. His place was taken on the Committee by his brother Jack. It is interesting to note that Frank later was to become an EAB missionary in 1949, and that Jack

Dyer's grandson, Roy, is today the Chairman of the EAB UK Committee.

7. Joys and Sorrows

Albert and Daisy Mundy were ecstatic when, after 15 years married, Daisy gave birth to a baby boy, Geraldo, on 2nd January 1943. Albert sent a cable to the Committee to give the news: *"January 2nd. Son Born today. All well. Albert Mundy"*. Another drought was biting hard in the Paraíba interior, support was hard to get through to them owing to the war, persecution was a constant, but God had given them a son. What a blessing!

However with Newsletter N° 26 came the news that the Mundys had gone to Recife in February and on the 17th Geraldo became very ill, but with prayer he recovered. They spent some days after this in the better climate of Garanhuns for Geraldo's sake. When they returned to Princesa they found that José Paulino has made some progress with the building of the church there, and had started doing some preaching and had won his sister-in-law for the Lord.

Then on 3rd July 1943 the Committee met to discuss the sad news received from Brazil in a cable: *"Geraldo passed away June 20th. Albert Mundy"*. The Committee replied immediately through Pastor Shearing: *"Our deepest sympathy and prayer. One Thessalonians four thirteen to eighteen from all at home. Winston Shearing"*. The Mundy's were devastated by their little boy's death, apparently caused by gastro enteritis and subsequent dehydration, and Albert's words in Prayer Letter 28 makes for moving reading:

"I must confess I have never found it so difficult to write in all my life as now. We have passed through the darkest and most trying experience. Our dear little Geraldo has been taken from us. The loss has been tremendous for us. Nevertheless we know the Lord never makes a mistake... but the empty cot, the wee things with which he loved to play, the soap box we made to serve as a pram, all knock hard against our hearts as they remind us of those few months so full of joy. How he loved to join in the meetings shouting out at the top of his little voice. We ask your prayers".

8. New Workers and New Church

Despite drought and death, with Daisy Mundy learning of her own mother's death later the same year on the Isle of Wight, the missionaries courageously stuck at their task and God turned 1943 into a year of victory for various reasons. First of all Albert Mundy appointed the first EAB national evangelist, José Soares, who was the son of the lady in Princesa that had been praying for a year for a pastor to come when the Mundys arrived, and a little later that same year another was added - none other than the converted assassin, José Paulino! Brother Mundy was greatly encouraged by this and commented: *"This is the best and surest way of getting the Gospel to the unsaved".*

Decisive in this turbulent period of crisis coupled with growth was the support the missionaries felt and received from the home supporters. The Committee was very active in raising funds, and battling to get them to Brazil despite all the wartime restrictions. The 5th EAB anniversary celebrations were held in no less than four churches. The first was at Southampton on 31st July, the second at Hardley Green on 14th August, the third at West Wellow on 21st August, and the fourth at Verwood on 28th August. This, and the Committee's frequent meetings, show the level of enthusiasm and support that EAB enjoyed.

Thus in Brazil the Mission continued maintaining two principal battle fronts: Princesa Isabel and Flores. In Princesa Isabel, as well as the regular services and evangelism, the team continued with the church building project, whilst maintaining their input to Flores 12 miles away over the border in Pernambuco State. On one such trip, six brethren, including Albert, walked the entire trip 12 miles each way because no transport was available. It is no wonder that God has blessed the more than 70 years of EAB with dedication and disposition like this.

Finally the great day arrived in Princesa Isabel when the first EAB church was ready for inauguration. At 2pm on Sunday, 17th

October 1943, a large crowd gathered outside the church and Albert Mundy says:

"We sang and prayed. I unlocked the door and we entered singing 'All hail the power of Jesus' Name'. Victory! Wonderful! Less than three years after entering Princesa we were rejoicing in this God given victory. The church filled to overflowing, being more outside than in. I spoke on 'victory'. Then the Mayor spoke and the Chief of Police and then many others. Eight came to Christ in the first week of services and six of these have remained firm in the Faith".
(Prayer Letter N° 29)

EAB never stood still to rest on any laurels following this landmark inauguration, and the following year Albert and the new workers José Soares and José Paulino were pressing 85 miles north to Serra Grande to transmit the Gospel of Christ in a new region of the State of Paraíba. God moved in this area and souls came to Christ. The work also continued in Flores despite severe drought, forcing some Christians to move away to survive, and more persecution.

More lasting encouragement of a family sort came on 17th August 1944 with the birth of Graham Mundy. When Graham went down with the same symptoms as the first child they had lost, the Mundys naturally felt very bewildered, and being more than due for a furlough decided to head for England, for a break. This of course was not as plain sailing as normal with the war still in progress, but in January 1945 Albert, Daisy and Graham Mundy set off on their way back to the UK. Graham was ill on the ship, but the ship's doctor took care of him and Graham pulled through.

9. First Furlough for EAB Pioneers

The Mundys landed at the Surrey Commercial Docks in London on 26th January 1945. They travelled by train to Southampton and were waiting at the bus station feeling very cold with Graham wrapped up in a blanket. Daisy remarked: *"We were frozen. The snow lay on the ground"*. Then somebody recognized them, and they were taken to the front of the queue for the bus which was to take them to the small village of Bramshaw, which was just inside the New Forest in Hampshire.

They didn't know quite where to go, as nobody knew when and where they would arrive under the circumstances of the war, so they knocked on the door of EAB Committee member, Stanley Dibden, who said, *"Whatever are you doing here? How we praised God to see a lovely fire, and they made up some beds for us to stay the night"*. The following day the Mundy's contacted Albert's parents, but they did not have room for them to stay there so they went to Awbridge, three miles north-west of Romsey, and stayed with the Hursts for their entire furlough. They were to stay for almost 20 months, and on 1st April 1946 they rejoiced at the birth of Ruth, a sister for Graham.

During their time in the UK, World War II thankfully came to an end, and Albert Mundy was engaged in an intense itinerant ministry speaking at 114 meetings in the first seven months, but he also kept in close contact with the Mission workers he had left behind in Brazil. Some news was good and others not so good. Reports from Princesa Isabel in 1945 were that the church was going well with large attendances, and two had come to Christ there in the early months of the year. The evangelists were visiting São José too, a village nine miles west of Princesa Isabel, but no decisions had been made there. From Flores came the bad news that the Christians had had to move away in search of work and even the little meeting place had been lost there. However better news came from Misericordia, known as Itaporanga today, where EAB's Manuel Soares entered to preach the Gospel for the first time on 30th May 1945. Today we have a thriving church in this place.

News came from EAB Evangelist José Paulino that he had finally found a small place to rent for services in Flores, but the local priest, João Amanço, had whipped up opposition to the letting with a crowd chanting at the small group of evangelicals, "We don't want the new sect here", and EAB lost the building. Later that same year even more persecution was reported to Albert Mundy from Brazil.

On 14th September 1946, EAB combined the 8th anniversary service with a farewell for Albert, Daisy, Graham and Ruth Mundy prior to their return to Brazil on 20th September. Clearly flying to Brazil was an enormous event for the EAB folk as Committee Member, E. Bergersen, makes clear in News Letter No. 6 of November 1946. I should mention that the numbering of EAB newsletters over the past more than 70 years has clearly been done to drive any researcher crazy! I imagine that the reason that EAB did not continue the numbering in the sequence it had up till the end of the first term of service for the Mundys, was because they thought numbering should start again with term two. Over the years the names of the news sheets have been changed as well, to add to the confusion. These things have been challenging, to say the least, in the gathering of information for this book!

However returning to E.Bergersen's account of the Mundy family's departure for Brazil, he tells us that Pastor Shearing, with Frank and Jack Dyer, went up to London to see them off. I will now leave the text exactly as Elgie Bergersen wrote it:

"Three parties of friends drew near to Heath Row Air Port, on Friday 20th September, at about 10.30 a.m. The Air Port is still only a temporary building although well appointed, and permission was obtained for all to gather in the waiting room before the Mundys cleared the Customs... we prayed together...Mr. Shearing says he will never forget Mr. Mundy and Mr. Mundy replies that it is harder to leave this time than it was the first time. There was a lump in the throat and silence...outside

the green grass stretches far and the Liner, like a great bird, the four triple blade propellers, the balloon tyres on the two front wheels, and the row of about a dozen portholes along the side. The Mundys come out, the door is under the wing, a few steps up and they enter".

The Mundys flew on the British South American Airways Lancastrian 'Star Speed' airplane. This transatlantic service had only started six months earlier. The Mundy family flew via Lisbon and Bathurst (today Banjul in West Africa's Gambia), and then to Natal in Rio Grande do Norte State in north-eastern Brazil. Albert Mundy's comment on the flight was, *"Arrived safely 5.50 p.m. on 21st September. The journey was quick is all that can be said about it. On the plane we could not sleep with the continual noise. We are fairly well, finding the heat very trying but Ruth is very sick. It has been too much for her."*

Source: RuthAS

10. A Thorny Way

A month later Albert Mundy wrote the following sad letter to Phyllis Hurst from Brazil:

"No doubt by now you have heard the heartbreaking news. We have sure been called to tread a thorny way. Poor little Ruth has been called away from us, dear little soul... suffered so patiently all the time. That is the thing that hurts so much...how she suffered! We had been back in Recife a month to the day and Ruth seemed so much better. Then all of a sudden she had a relapse. We have tried to understand but we are perplexed to say the least. Graham awoke this morning and asked, 'Where is baby mum'? It cuts to the quick when he asks, 'Where is Tati gone'? You will I now understand how much we are in need of prayer these days".

The Mundys had been again devastated by the loss of a child, but they dragged themselves back to the interior after this to get back into the work of the Mission for God. Culture and climate shock is evident in all they write at this time. Daisy writes about *"millions of mosquitoes"*, and Albert talks about Graham's ill health and it being tough going in Princesa Isabel. Now their luggage was finally arriving, but they had to pay extra for it and some of it was damaged.

However there was a positive side to things and Graham was picking up Portuguese very quickly as children do. *"He is growing now"*, Daisy comments, *"and he loves to sing"*. Their reports talk about progress at Serra Grande, Misericordia, Gameleira and Sítio Coxos. One 20 year old woman was beaten up badly by her family trying to force her to leave the Lord, but the girl resisted and was now requesting baptism! EAB's field of action was clearly expanding and being consolidated, and they start to talk about the need for a vehicle to help them cope with all the demands upon them.

In his September 1947 letter Albert Mundy speaks of his desire to reach Conceição with the Gospel that year as it is still unreached.

"We need more workers! The labourers are few", he exclaims. Gladly today EAB has a good church in Conceição; well established in the centre of town. Albert goes on to say that at least EAB has increased its missionary force through the purchase of Dorcas, which turns out to be a mule, but £305 had now been sent to Brazil as a 'Gospel Car Fund' so soon EAB would soon be on four wheels!

By November 1947 Albert had been able to purchase a vehicle and he clearly started making up for lost time by travelling extensively and visiting places he had never been able to visit before. He was also planning on moving the Mission's headquarters to Patos as it was a larger town in a more strategic position for further expansion of ministry. Mr. Mundy visited Patos, and soon found an appropriate house to live in and was now looking for a building to rent in which to hold services.

Meanwhile in Princesa Isabel a new wave of blessing was felt which greatly encouraged the missionaries as 18 came to Christ, and a baptism held in a lake attracted such a crowd that the local priest's procession for the same time had hardly anyone in it!

11. New Headquarters and New Missionaries

On 13th May 1948 EAB moved its field headquarters to Patos, a town with a population of 12,176 at the time, which is situated 93 miles north-east of Princesa Isabel. This was an intelligent move by Albert Mundy, because Patos has a strategic central position as regards the interior of Paraíba, whilst being close to both Pernambuco and Rio Grande do Norte States. Patos has been EAB's base ever since as a consequence.

On visits to Patos, leading up to the move there, Albert Mundy made contacts with a few Christians that had gathered there from another area, and he rented a house in advance and a meeting hall to start a church. Thus the EAB Patos church started with Albert, Daisy and Graham Mundy, who brought with them from Princesa Isabel a young woman called Xandu Soares. This foursome linked up with three young Christians who had been converted through the ministry of two American missionaries, who worked in the Acauã rural area of Prata County in the State of Paraíba, a good distance south of Patos, and were known to Albert. These three young Christians were important figures in the young Patos church, and were a brother and sister, Cesário de Paula Conserva and his sister Maria, together with her husband Inácio. Inácio became the first leader of the little Patos church whenever Albert went away on preaching journeys, and when he and his wife moved away to the State of Bahia to find work, it was Cesário that took on the local leadership role. Josinete, present day worker with EAB in Patos, is a daughter of Inácio and Maria. The four from Princesa Isabel, and the three from Prata, were soon joined by a widower called Clementino and his four children, Erminha, Maria José, Eunice and Paulo.

Thus the new EAB church at Patos started with seven adults and three children, including the missionary family, and it started in a street near the river in a far from ideal location, but it was all that could be afforded and found at the time. The street near the river was so full of mosquitoes that it was known as "Mosquito Street", but eventually this street's name was changed to "Espinharas

Street", after the name of the nearby river which flows through Patos when there is enough rainfall.

One of these founder members, Cesário, of the EAB Patos church comments on those early days in Patos in 1948:

"It wasn't easy to be an evangelical Christian in Patos in 1948. I had only got converted, at 19 years of age, the previous year, but I had seen the light of the truth of God's Word and refused to be thwarted by the persecution, opposition and prejudice against us which we met everywhere.

In those days there was no electricity in Patos from the national grid and we depended on an erratic generator run by the Council which constantly failed. Hence whenever we went to the more distant boroughs of Patos like São Sebastião, Vila Cavalcanti, Vitória, Jatobá, Monte Castelo and Mata Burro (known today as Liberdade), we took a paraffin lamp with us to start up whenever necessary. In those days we walked for miles preaching the Gospel in Patos and surrounding region but we always carried a lamp.

I lived off making sweets in a back yard factory and later my half-brother Zacarias joined us in Patos and he, together with my brother-in-law Roberto, who married my sister Sebastiana, became salesmen for the "factory". Let me tell you that the "factory' was basically a very primitive giant cauldron which we heated on a wood fire. I used to get through a 60 kilo sack of sugar a day and we sold a sweet for a "tostão. We were poor but we made ends meet and we were happy in the Lord. Slowly these and other members of my family came to know the Lord and became active in the church. Zacarias became an evangelist with EAB for over 40 years till the day he died. Roberto was an EAB evangelist for many years too".

At around this time people in the UK were starting to respond to Bert Mundy's cry for help and for more workers in north-east Brazil, and the Committee announced a list of candidates being considered: Mr. and Mrs. W. Hartley, Miss I. Chapman (who in October 1948 became Ivy Dyer having married Frank Dyer who was back on the Committee having returned from the war), Mr. G. Emmens and Mr. B. Snelgrove. It was stated that others were known to be considering missionary service with EAB too. Then in the new style six-monthly July 1948 GTB News Bulletin it was definitely announced by the committee that Ivy Chapman, Bernard Snelgrove, Gordon Emmens and Frank Dyer were to go to Brazil with EAB. Bernard W. Snelgrove was the first to leave, and his farewell service was held at the Ringwood Road Mission Hall, Totton, Southampton on 20th December 1948. In the second edition of the News Bulletin Bernard W. Snelgrove was announced as "The First Recruit" having arrived in Brazil on 27th January 1949, four days before I was born.

Bernard played the piano accordion, and was soon involved with Albert Mundy and Frank Dyer (who arrived in Brazil about two months after Bernard), in travelling in ministry to different mission outposts. In a News Letter of mid-1949 Bernard's description of his first "long Gospel journey" to Jasmine in the State of Pernambuco makes interesting reading:

"In the first stage I was shocked to find that the truck was already packed with 50 people and their luggage. However somehow we found room for our baggage and pushed ourselves into the centre of the truck...at every turn in the road; at each bump over a large pothole, or swerve around a rock in the track, everyone fell on the person nearest them, but being a jolly crowd no one cared...As we climbed up the narrow, winding, rough and dangerous track, zigzagging up the mountain side, I took a look back into the plain below, in which Patos is situated. It was a lovely sight, for Patos is encircled by mountains, and it was easy to understand why it is so hot there...but later away in the woods we held meetings on Wednesday and Thursday and two listening accepted the Lord Jesus".

We cannot move on with EAB history without registering a date and event of great importance that happened on 8th September 1949. For at the address cited above, from where Bernard Snelgrove wrote his letter, Elizabeth Louisa Dyer was born. Her mother, Ivy Dyer, had come already pregnant to Brazil and

Elizabeth, or Liz as I call her, or Betinha as most call her in Brazil–who was to marry me in Southampton a little over 20 years later–made her entrance into the world and EAB and ACEV (the Brazilian national evangelical denomination founded by EAB), with whom she has faithfully served the Lord ever since. To sum up Elizabeth in a nutshell is no easy task. As a child she survived smallpox without any medical help. She could soon speak Portuguese better than her parents and used to do the shopping at six years of age. She had an ovary removed at 13, and that same year she was already teaching a Sunday School class of 120 children. Elizabeth is an amazingly dedicated missionary and Christian with a commitment to God, EAB/ACEV and north-east Brazil as I have never seen in anyone else. Everyone likes Betinha. She is a gift of God. She rightly is co-director of EAB today. In fact she is streets ahead of me.

Elizabeth's parents, Frank and Ivy Dyer, had sailed for Brazil early in 1949. They left Tilbury Docks on 28th February on the S.S. Boniface which was a cargo ship which took just six passengers; so a different ship altogether to that which first brought the Mundys with well over a thousand passengers. Being a cargo ship it made many stops and took a full month to arrive at the Recife docks in Brazil on 29th March 1949. Albert Mundy was there to meet them.

Frank was born at Holbury in Hampshire on 9th July 1916, and Ivy at Blackfield close by, on 24th May 1923. They were married on 2nd October 1948 at Blackfield. Frank served in the Royal Artillery and the Rifle Brigade in World War II, seeing action in both Africa and Italy and receiving the George Cross for bravery, though prior to this he had been one of the founder members of the EAB UK Home Committee. Now Frank, together with his wife, went to the front lines with a different army.

The Dyers were initially installed in the Mission House in Patos together with the Mundys and Bernard Snelgrove, and on 22nd April 1949, leaving his pregnant wife behind with Daisy Mundy, Frank set out on his first evangelistic journey with Albert and Bernard to minister.

The first thing that did not impress Frank, he remarked in a handwritten letter in our archives, was the lack of punctuality on the part of the lorry driver that agreed to take them, together with eight other passengers and cargo. He had guaranteed to leave at 6am but in fact left at 5pm. Owing to the late departure they all had to sleep the night at Coremas, some 56 miles west of Patos, in a public dormitory whose owner had the audacity to call it a "hotel"! Hammocks were strung up side-by-side and all the men slept like this in the entrance hall. There was not much room for fidgeting! At dawn, after a cup of strong sweet coffee, they were on their way along the very bumpy roads again. Despite a burst tyre, and the crossing of two rivers, they covered the 35 miles to Boqueirão dos Cochos (today called Igaracy) by midday, but had to walk the last four miles to get to the farmstead where they were being expected. *"In their way they received us as royal guests and made us feel very welcome",* Frank commented. He then said that at night Bernard played the accordion, he himself spoke through an interpreter, and Albert both convened and spoke. They taught them a new chorus which was a Brazilian version of "Keep your eyes on God". The team stayed at this place for three days ministering to a total of 50 people, before moving on another 26 miles up a mountain range to Serra Grande, where Albert Mundy had pioneered ministry since 1943, travelling on horses, donkeys and mules.

Having left early they arrived at the São José Community in the Serra Grande Mountains by lunch time, and it is interesting to note that Frank Dyer mentions that they ate at a blind man's house, because descendents of this man were to take part in the founding of the EAB church at Campina Grande decades later. Lunch had been coffee, roast corn on the cob and sugar cane. Later the team moved on to Gamalheira Community where a service was held at night with 60 present. The following morning they travelled on to the Panelas Community where they held three services and baptized nine in a lake. Following their stay at Panelas, the team went back to São José to hold two services and in the evening service *"about 100 gathered to hear the Gospel and there were several decisions".*

It should be mentioned that it was in July 1949, that Conceição was reached with the Gospel by EAB for the first time. This town, 30 miles south-west of Itaporanga, reacted adversely to the evangelical presence as usual with stone throwing and hostility. Despite this, EAB workers preached on for four days and seven came to Christ.

In October 1949 Bernard Snelgrove issued his Prayer Letter no.6 from Coronel Antônio Pessoa Street, Nº 583, in Patos. This street is called Prado Street today and it is in this street, at number 409 that the EAB church was built in the early 1960s, and there it stands to this day. In his letter Bernard describes a journey in August, with Albert, to minister at Conceição and Misericórdia (today Itaporanga), and another in October with Frank Dyer to minister at Jasmin in the State of Pernambuco.

It is clear from Frank Dyer's early letters from Brazil that he felt immediately at home in the Brazilian interior. He commented about how he was impressed, as he travelled with Albert Mundy, by how many little congregations had already been founded, often in the most out of the way places. Jasmin, a rural community in the County of Tabira in Pernambuco State was clearly a place close to Frank's heart, and he built a little church building there in the 1950s.

However as Christmas approached in 1949, the missionaries were excited because EAB managed to purchase a small terraced house in the more central street called 'Coronel Antônio Pessoa', known today as 'Rua do Prado'. This house was transformed into a meeting hall, in the same street where the EAB church is today, and only about 100 metres from the present day site. Albert, Frank, José Paulino, and various other local Christians, worked for three weeks knocking out the internal walls of the house so as to make it into a meeting hall; putting on a new roof, and generally cleaning it up and painting it to make it into a church. It was a big job, and the missionaries were determined to get it finished for the Christmas Convention starting on Saturday 24th December because all events are celebrated on the eve of the event in Brazil. Many nights the team worked till 11 o'clock at night by the light of paraffin pressure lamps, and Frank Dyer comments: "*I must admit that with the heat of the day and the late nights I found it very tiring*". On the Thursday before Christmas, 18 Christians arrived ready for the Christmas Convention; from Itaporanga, Serra Grande and Boqueirão dos Coxos. Then on the Friday others arrived, including seven from Jasmin in Pernambuco State, and in all there were 32 people from other towns and villages to put up for Christmas! "*This is what Christmas is all about*", thought Frank Dyer! Thus at 3pm on Christmas Eve they jubilantly inaugurated the first EAB owned church building in Patos.

Albert Mundy made a Christmas tree for this great day, using local wood and sisal, and we still have this tree to this day, and we still maintain the tradition started that Christmas. When time came for the evening service all the Sunday School children sat round the tree in Church and received little gifts. Then on Christmas Day morning all gathered again around God's Word, and in the afternoon they walked down to the river to baptize eight new converts. What a lovely Christmas present for Jesus! However anti-protestant feelings were high in Patos, and as the good number of evangelical Christians walked towards the river, many booed them, and others hooted and jeered. Frank's army tent, used as a changing room, had to be guarded because there were people there to really cause trouble, but clearly some of them were moved, and as the baptism progressed many were touched by God. Then the fifth and final service of the Convention was held at night back in the new church, and what a crowd gathered. The EAB church was now the talk of the town and many could not even get into the church as it filled to capacity.

The GTB News Bulletin N° 4 of January 1950 shows a photo of Bernard with the Mundys and Dyers taken in April the previous year and that, as far as the EAB archives are concerned, is the last we hear of Bernard Snelgrove in EAB.

Albert Mundy reported in early 1950 that there were now 20 adult members in the Patos church, plus 18 children and teenagers all committed to Christ. Princesa Isabel was not going so well however, but on the other hand a new church plant had been started in the Pernambuco town of Tabira, and the missionaries had also preached for the first time at Afogados de Ingazeira in the same state. Albert and Frank also went ministering at a place called "Desert" which would seem to be the same place with this name where EAB, 57 years later, drilled a well in 2007. God is faithful!

When the missionaries went again to minister at Serra Grande, in late February 1950, they found none of the men at home for the service because two of their donkeys and a number of their goats had been killed by wild cats so the men had all gone to hunt them! However word spread that Albert, Frank and José Paulino had arrived so the hunters returned to join some lovely services over the weekend, including a baptism of new believers, one of which had accepted the Lord in 1943 when Albert Mundy first preached at Serra Grande. In April, that year, Frank and Albert spent some time ministering at Itaporanga, and Frank was improving sufficiently in Portuguese to be able consider moving to Princesa Isabel, where the work was not going so well, with his wife Ivy and daughter Elizabeth.

12. Further Reinforcements

Back in the UK, the January 1950 EAB News Bulletin No. 4 announced that new EAB missionary candidates were engaged in deputation work preparing to join EAB in Brazil. Mary and James Peasley were visiting churches in Lancashire and Jacqueline and Gordon Emmens were doing the same in Northern Ireland. Edition No. 5 announced the farewell service for both couples on 15th June at the Central Hall, Southampton, and a brief report by E. Bergersen, of the EAB UK Committee, later said the service was "splendid". He went on to say that 30 supporters had made the journey to Liverpool Docks on 12th July 1950 to see them on to the small, but new, 2,990 ton S.S. Dennis, which sailed for Brazil the next day. Albert Mundy met the new missionaries off the ship in Recife on 1st August, and they got through customs with no problem as Albert was now an experienced negotiator in these matters! They immediately set off on the 275 mile journey to Patos, where once settled in they launched in to studying the Portuguese language. From what I am told it was the experienced missionaries that taught the newcomers, which with hindsight was not a good idea, because inevitably everybody acquired the same pronunciation and grammatical errors, as well as limited vocabulary. I avoided this in 1972 by doing a deal with a university Portuguese teacher. He taught me Portuguese and I taught him English, though my teacher, Badu, taught me much more than I taught him! I also had the advantage of a Brazilian-born wife which none of the earlier missionaries had. If the learner is a linguistic parrot, like I am, it is essential that you are copying the right people!

Prior to the four new missionaries' arrival in Patos on 29th May 1950, Frank and Ivy Dyer felt confident enough in the language and culture to move to Princesa Isabel and take on the responsibilities of the church there, which was clearly missing the Mundys since they had moved from there to Patos. It was just as well that the Dyers did move out of the Mission base in Patos, as the small house, which still stands today, would never have squeezed everyone in, even though Bernard Snelgrove had ended his service with EAB.

Bernard Snelgrove only worked with EAB for just over a year, returning to UK on 27th March 1950. He later returned to Brazil to work in the south-east, and is now over 80 years of age, living in Belo Horizonte in the State of Minas Gerais which is about 1,500 miles south of Patos, so he certainly didn't leave EAB because he didn't like Brazil. Since I have been in Brazil I have met Bernard twice. Once was when he visited us in Patos in 1972, and the other was when Liz and I visited him in Teófilo Otoni, Minas Gerais; when we also visited Mrs. Roult of the Peniel Chapel Missionary Society and her daughter Eliad.

It was Divine providence that Frank Dyer moved at this point to Princesa Isabel, because not long afterwards the principal early national evangelist, José Paulino, who had carried on in the leadership of the work at Princesa Isabel between Albert's move to Patos and Frank's arrival, became ill with gall bladder complications and died. Of course in those days, especially in the interior, gall bladder stones, which today are resolved with key-hole surgery, were a major issue of life and death.

When Frank realized how ill Evangelist José Paulino was he sent a telegram to Albert Mundy asking him to go to Princesa Isabel immediately. The problem was, however, that Albert Mundy was away preaching up in the Serra Grande area, some 95 miles west of Patos and 85 miles north-west of Princesa Isabel where he was needed. When Daisy received the telegram in Patos she sensed the urgency of the hour, and a young man from the Patos church, who had a "fine horse", agreed to take off in search of Albert and give him the telegram. When the rider caught up with Albert Mundy it was 4pm, and Albert was waiting for a couple to arrive to marry them. Upon receiving the telegram, which read *"José Paulino very sick. No hope held for him"*, Albert felt it very much as this was the brother who had been with him since 1941, and helped him build the Princesa church and had stuck with him "through thick and thin". Though José Soares was mentioned in reports as the first national evangelist, and shortly afterwards José Paulino became one too, it is clear that little more was heard about José Soares, but José Paulino was involved in the work everywhere. What a transformation had occurred in this man's life, turning from killer to Christ!

Albert called the couple to be married urgently, preached to them and married them, and then was off into the night heading for Misericórdia (Itaporanga) with a group of brethren. They reached Misericórdia at dawn hoping to find a brother who would get them a change of horses, but he had gone to a place called Ranchinho further along the road, so Albert pressed on, reaching there at 10am. They had something to eat, changed horses, and then rode really hard all day, in the direction of Princesa until they could keep going no longer, and stopped to sleep at 9pm. However they arose very early, drunk coffee, saddled the horses, and then they were off again desperately trying to get to Princesa before it was too late. Albert knew that burials take place very quickly after death in Brazil so when he arrived at 10pm in Princesa he was so happy to find José Paulino alive and lucid, *"though very sick"*. Albert was able to talk to him, he prayed and read the Word with him and sang many hymns chosen by José Paulino.

José Paulino brightened up with Albert's arrival and slept well that night, but the following morning he had a relapse. He realized he was dying and called someone to whom he gave instructions about things that needed doing, and even gave the measurements for his coffin. *"I sat with him"*, says Albert in his report, *"and he told me he would not last the night. I sat there watching... sometimes praying, sometimes reading the Word, sometimes singing hymns. Then he asked me to greet Daisy with the Peace of the Lord when I saw her next... and one after another he wished everyone farewell looking forward to seeing Jesus in His beauty. He then asked if there was anyone who he had not spoken to, and there was one non-Christian called Joaquim. I called him over and José Paulino said to him 'Goodbye my old friend Joaquim. Accept the Lord Jesus as your Saviour. He is the only way of Salvation'! The poor man could not answer. The word went home! I thought how grand that he preached to the last the old old story of God's redeeming grace. At five to ten that night he asked us to read the Word again and Frank turned to Revelation chapter five, and as Frank read the last verse José Paulino passed into the presence of the King of Kings. I have never seen a greater victory!"*

Everyone then joined in singing the hymn, "By the throne of God is prepared a place for thee", though Albert comments that there were many a lump in the throat and few dry eyes. Then José Paulino's widow, Rosa, gave their testimony of God's transforming love and power saying she was more of a believer now than she ever had been.

Crowd leaves Princesa Isabel church at José Paulino's funeral

Albert Mundy felt deeply the loss of co-worker José Paulino, at just 43 years of age, and yet commented: *"I have lost the brother I loved more than any other in Brazil...he has gone to his reward. We took him to the church he worked so hard to build and it was a glorious service with crowds inside and out. José Paulino has gone on but his testimony remains.*

After this we stayed in Princesa a few days and then I went to speak at Flores before spending three days preaching at Carnaíba, also in Pernambuco State, then at Tabira and Jasmin on the way back to Patos. We had travelled over 400 miles, married a couple, buried a brother, preached to many and baptized four".

13. The Truth Marches On

On 23rd September 1950, the four EAB missionary families all set off for an evangelical conference at Serra Grande, where a series of services over a period of days were greatly blessed of God, and nine new converts were baptized. It must have been quite a test for the newly arrived Peasleys and Emmens, not two months in the country, especially for the men to wear suits and ties in the terrific heat, as well as still adjusting to the food, coping with no toilets and understanding little Portuguese. A baptism of fire indeed!

The Serra Grande 1950 Conference: (left to right – front row) Xandu Soares from Patos, Gordon & Jacqueline Emmens, Daisy and Albert Mundy (with Graham, aged six, in front of Albert), Frank and Ivy Dyer (with Elizabeth, aged one, on Ivy's lap), and Mary & Albert Peasley. On the second row back, behind Frank, is Cesário de Paula from Patos; on the same row, behind Albert, is Antônio Ferreira from Itaporanga whom we called "31" because he had that number of children; on the same row, behind Daisy, is Israel Martins from Serra Grande.

In 1951 the new missionaries were feeling their feet, and so the four families were able to multiply mission fire power by going to minister in different areas at one time. Frank and Ivy were happy to give Elizabeth a baby brother, Samuel, born 15th March 1951, at Princesa Isabel, where their ministry continued. In passing I must say how difficult it can be to be a missionary kid! The Brazilian

Christians expect them to be perfect, and to settle in the UK later in life is far from easy. However going back to Princesa Isabel, Frank continued to be very active in ministry and even cycled to Flores and Carnaíba, in Pernambuco State, to preach the Gospel. This meant five and a half hours on the bike each way!

The Peasleys moved to Conceição and established themselves there to consolidate the work of EAB in the area, and the Emmens were also clearly looking to move elsewhere, as they eventually did to the State of Ceará. Gordon Emmens was helping in Patos still in 1951 as Albert Mundy often travelled round the growing field. Albert worked a lot in Misericórdia (Itaporanga) during this year as the Christians needed support in the face of profuse provocation and persecution. One night in a prayer meeting the local nuns sent a group of girls from their school into the meeting hall with a sack of torn up Bibles and emptied it in the middle of the hall whilst the believers were at prayer. It was a shock to all and brought great sadness at seeing God's Word destroyed in such a way.

Frank Dyer reported ministry in Tavares in October 1951 though he found it very hard going there. Then in November that year he ministered in Manaíra which he described as *"a remote place"* but where people were more interested in the Gospel. Frank says that the late EAB Evangelist, José Paulino, had ministered in Manaíra in 1947 or 1948.

The year 1952 brought about a series of changes in the EAB missionary jigsaw puzzle, with only the Peasleys remaining where they were previously at Conceição. Their ministry was proving fruitful, and Mary Peasley's midwifery qualifications were coming into great use and building bridges with the people. The Dyers moved back to Patos, in preparation for the Mundys going on furlough towards the end of the year, and the Emmens finally defined their field of ministry opening up courageous doors of service in the Roman Catholic strongholds of the State of Ceará. Initially Gordon Emmens visited the State with Albert Mundy, and then the Emmens moved to Missão Velha in Ceará State where they received a very hostile reception. The problems seem to have gotten worse when, of the only seven that would go to their services, three made decisions for Christ! This led the local priest to whip up aggressive action against them, and they found themselves with their backs to the wall with lots of shouting at them and some stones starting to be thrown. At this point the local head of the post office stepped in to avoid bloodshed and called in the Chief of Police to escort them to safety in the Post Office. However, whilst this was going on the priest himself went and broke into the Emmens house, wrecked havoc, and made two bonfires outside with their furniture! A warm welcome indeed to Ceará! Despite this, and at times under police protection, the Emmens resisted and stood firm and very slowly, but surely, saw a group of 11 coming to Christ at Missão Velha.

In the second half of 1952 Ivy Dyer very nearly died with typhoid. She had a high fever for over three weeks and was delirious for six days. The doctors despaired with her case, but God undertook and brought her back from the brink. Then on 13th November the Mundys travelled to Britain for their second furlough on the H.M.S. Alcantara. Frank Dyer, Gordon Emmens and Albert Peasley were all there to see them off at Recife and were allowed on board before the ship set sail. Frank became acting Field Superintendent during Albert's absence. The Mundys were welcomed back to the UK by a good crowd on Monday 24th November 1952, at Southampton Docks.

In 1953 it was Jacqueline Emmens's turn to go down with typhoid, (working with her husband in the State of Ceará), but it would seem that she was able to obtain the correct medication, and gratefully recovered quicker than Ivy Dyer did. Another important historical fact from this year was when Frank appointed Zacarias Salvador to be the leader of the work at Itaporanga. This brother was to be an evangelist with EAB for over 40 years from then on. Reports from this year show the Peasleys continuing at Conceição and the Emmens in Ceará State (though having moved from Missão Velha to Juazeiro do Norte), with the Dyers based at Patos, but with Frank travelling to the normal list of works established by EAB at Princesa Isabel (where the work was tough going again); plus Itaporanga and the Serra Grande area. Clearly Tabira and

Afogados de Ingazeira in Pernambuco State were regularly visited too, despite Friar Damião's opposition trying to hinder this. Frank Dyer did manage to be back in Patos on 27th November 1953, for the birth of his third child, David. The baby was very ill for some days, and Ivy told me she was only able to see him after nine days, but he pulled through.

In 1954 Gordon and Jacqueline Emmens moved to another town in the State of Ceará, called Crato, where they stuck at the job in an extremely idolatrous and spiritually dark area; which Albert Peasley refers to at one point as, *"the most difficult field in Brazil today owing to the extreme fanaticism of the Roman Catholics"*. It was in the early part of 1954 that Elizabeth Dyer, at just four years of age, started to travel round the field with her father. First Elizabeth went with her father to Princesa Isabel and then to Itaporanga. Frank comments, *"Elizabeth soon made friends with everyone there and did not give me any trouble"*. Elizabeth also went to Flores with her father with *"her likeable manner winning the affection of the people and the proprietor of a fruit preserving factory gave her two tins of guava which did please her"!* To this day Elizabeth has the same nature and way with the people. She is a great asset to EAB.

One of the founder members of the EAB Patos church, Cesário de Paula Conserva, who is over 80 years old today, and still living in the State capital João Pessoa, tells us that at about this time the Patos church was progressing slowly, but surely. The more central meeting hall in Prado Street was more conducive to growth and the small group of Christians was very active. They had services every night in some part of the town and always carried Tilley lamps with them in case of power cuts, as the local generated electricity was not trustworthy. Thus many evenings the band of EAB Christians would walk three to six miles each way to hold services in the Patos boroughs of São Sebastião, Vila Cavalcanti, Vitória, Jatobá, Monte Castelo and Mata Burro. The latter borough is today called Liberdade. Then Cesário went on:

"I especially remember Antônio Ferreira getting converted in this period, together with his wife, Rosa. He could play the piano

accordion and soon became a real help in the work as well as being a great story teller with a great sense of humour. However one incident with Antônio stands out in my memory. The service was coming to a close with the last hymn and Antônio was playing his accordion sat on a wooden stool. The pastor then asked him to close in prayer so he stood up to pray. However the stool was old and cracked and the cracked part clamped on to his trousers! Thus he was stood there praying with an accordion sticking out at the front of him and a stool sticking out at the back! We did laugh at the end of the meeting and all the way walking home. Those were happy days. We were all very poor but were very happy and totally committed to Jesus. Our life was Jesus and the church. We lived for nothing else.

Some of the brethren and me then decided we needed to reach out to neighbouring towns and villages on Saturdays and we felt led to start with Cacimba de Aréia, 16 miles south-east of Patos by road. We used to get there on the market trucks and do personal evangelism throughout the day, building up to a service in the evening. However the thing was that the truck carrying the people home from market left late afternoon so every time we went we had to walk home to Patos after the evening service. We used to follow the bed of the River Farinha because that is a shorter route than the road and it is impossible to get lost like that in the dark of night. When it was a full moon it was lovely but when there was no moon it was pretty dark and spooky. There was always the possibility of treading on a snake, meeting a wolf or wild cat, or being held up by bandits, but, apart from a few close shaves, those long walks home were joyful times of chatting, listening to Antonio Ferreira's stories, much laughter and much singing praise to God. Looking back it seems amazing that we did this so often – almost crazy! However at the time it was just wonderful serving the Lord and spreading the Gospel in this way.

When Pastor Frank and Pastor Eduardo (Albert Mundy was known as Eduardo in Brazil) *got jeeps then we were able to reach out further to places like Passagem, in the same general direction as Cacimba de Aréia, but 22 miles from Patos.*

I remember going to Serra Grande with the pastors once too and we held a service at Brother Israel's house. This brother ran a sort of shop in his front room. That was how you did it in those days, and his shop sold farming implements like primitive hoes, knives and machetes. I remember how many machetes there were all over the floor that night! Well, during the service a group of men gathered just to ridicule us and poke fun and they started to tell Sister Xandu, who was playing her accordion, for her to speed up the music as they wanted to dance! This happened with every hymn until Israel could take it no longer so when the hymn ended he stepped forward to speak. 'Look', he said, 'I'm a Christian and proud of it'! All of us responded with a loud amen. Then Israel continued, 'but you see those machetes in there? They are not converted!' There was total silence! But the group of trouble makers got the message and left immediately because they knew Israel was a tough guy who had been very violent before accepting Christ in his life and they weren't about to take any chances"!

Finally the return of Albert, Daisy and Graham Mundy was announced for March 1955. Life went at a different pace in those days and as travelling was so much slower, so furloughs tended to be much longer than today. Their farewell service was announced for Friday 25th March 1955, at the Central Hall, Southampton at 7.30 p.m. Who would go to an event like this on a Friday evening in this day and age? They sailed back on their old friend, H.M.S. Alcantara, leaving Southampton on 30th March. Back in Brazil Albert Mundy held a week's meetings in Patos, and then set off to Itaporanga to visit the church and mentioned the need to buy land to build a church there. He also preached for the first time at the Mozelo Community in the County of Olho D'Água in Paraíba State where 60 gathered to hear the preaching of God's Word. Upon returning to Patos Albert wrote, *"We found that Brother Dyer's family had increased with the addition of a daughter and both mother and baby are doing fine"*. That was Eunice, born in Patos on 27th May, 1955. Albert also went on to talk about the Tabira work being well established as well as Jasmin, in the rural area of the same county, but to get back to Patos he had to travel a lot of the way on an ox cart! Patos *"now has a population of*

17,000", he commented. Today, in 2012, that population has grown to a little over 100,000.

In September 1955, Albert Peasley announced how happy he was to see the Mundy's back, and that they had brought back from the UK new loudspeaker equipment which they had used at Conceição for the first time, and the whole town heard the Gospel as a result! Albert Peasley also mentioned the successful purchase of land to build a church and that the building was to start that very week.

EAB policy was for missionaries to serve five year terms of service before having a break, or furlough, back in the UK. Thus the Dyers were by now overdue for their turn, and boarded the good old H.M.S. Alcantara on Elizabeth Dyer's 6th birthday, 8th September 1955, a day on which she tasted ice cream for the first time in her life!

The Dyer family going for their first furlough in 1955

The EAB Committee decided to hold back the 17th Anniversary Service that year to 24th September to allow for the arrival of the Dyer family on the 19^{th,} who were unexpectedly joined by Jacqueline Emmens and her son Malcolm who were in need of healthcare, thus bringing them to the UK ahead of what had been planned for them. Jacqueline Emmens went home first with the baby in July and Gordon followed later, arriving in England on 12th September. Thus the 24th September service was both the AGM and a double welcome home meeting.

Meanwhile Albert Mundy went to Jasmin, in Pernambuco, to see the church that Frank had built there in his absence. We still have, with Frank's handwriting, the plans he drew up for the church building. Albert commented, *"Last week I made a trip to Jasmin. The church building is completed, and it now only lacks the pews. It looks very nice indeed, and the local brethren are delighted with the results. Praise God"!* Then Brother Mundy went on to give some more good news in that EAB had been able to purchase some land in Patos to build a proper church building at a cost of 14 Contos, the Brazilian currency of the time. He said this was roughly £70. This land, in a good central position in town, is the site where the current EAB church building is standing to this day.

Not long after returning from his second furlough, Albert Mundy was also blazing the trail in new towns and villages previously untouched by the Gospel. Firstly at Coremas, then at Santa Terezinha and thirdly a community called Mina de Ouro, all in the State of Paraíba.

Albert and Mary Peasley had become the parents of two children during their five years in Brazil. The first was a boy, whom they named Ian, and the second was a girl, whom they named Hazel, born in May 1955. Hazel was born physically handicapped, and certainly needed treatment that could not be obtained in the interior of Brazil's north-east. I can imagine that this situation put a lot of strain on the Peasleys, and Pastor Winston Shearing of the EAB UK Committee wrote in the GTB News of May 1956, that the Peasleys felt their need of a change, and they needed to return home *"both for themselves and the children as soon as possible"*.

Thus on 16th June 1956, Albert, Mary, Ian and Hazel Peasley set sail on the old faithful H.M.S Alcantara arriving at Southampton on the 27th. Suddenly three of the four missionary families were all in England at the same time, only leaving the founders holding the fort back in Brazil.

14. Tensions amongst the EAB Workforce

This morning I had breakfast with Ivy Dyer, approaching her 85th birthday in Patos, and told her where I had got up to in writing this history of EAB. I told her that I was now about to write about a difficult period that EAB went through in the mid-1950s, over the delicate issue of the distribution of funds amongst the four missionary families. *"Oh"*, Ivy responded immediately, *"There was always trouble over money from the start. Frank didn't receive a penny from EAB during the first year until he had spent all his personal savings he brought out with him"!*

This reaction is symptomatic of the rumbling disagreements and discontentment that existed within the EAB ranks once its workforce multiplied from 1949 onwards. That problems arise in any organization is inevitable, but it is how you handle the problems is the crucial point, and I think EAB eventually sorted this issue out fairly well.

Reflecting on EAB history thus far it is easy to see that the first decade was plain sailing as far as funding missionaries because there was only one family involved. Of course, they endured incredible difficulties in the war years in receiving money at all, and the fact is, mission leaders are always under so much pressure in developing countries anyway–there is always more to do and never enough money to do it! However, that is different to tensions and strife between missionaries, and clearly the second decade of EAB's history was the crisis period in which this had to be sorted out.

For a small Mission coping with four new missionary families within 18 months (between 1949 and 1950) this was a gigantic challenge at the least. This is talking about a 400% increase involving the need for a gigantic growth in income, plus all the logistics involved in such growth. There were missionaries galore to learn the language, feed, house, and slowly make them useful, involving them in the work. Also, during this period the missionaries had a total of seven children to add to the calculations! With hindsight it is clear that too many missionaries came too quickly, and on 20th July 1955 Albert Mundy was writing in a personal letter that, *"Frank works well with me but it will be a good thing when we are fewer on the field"*.

There clearly was a lot of debate going on behind the scenes concerning how to administer the tensions that had arisen, but we don't have the committee's minutes till July 1964 onwards and we do not have access to other private letters we know exist, so it is difficult to arrive at conclusions. One letter we do have was written by Frank Dyer to the Committee and Albert Mundy on 19th November, but Frank forgot to put the year. However, the fact that it was addressed to the Committee and Albert together presumably means that it was written whilst Albert was on furlough in 1954, and this is confirmed by other contents of the letter. In the letter Frank makes it clear that the "distribution of finance" is something that is not *"helping the fellowship between the workers. I don't see how the present system of dividing it up can ever be done in a peaceful way. It tends to make each one criticize the others. Whilst Gordon Emmens and Albert Peasley were here in Patos the fellowship became marred through this"*. Apparently Gordon had argued that he should receive more because he paid rent where he lived whereas Albert Peasley did not. Gordon also complained that he had not received extra to cover expenses when his wife had typhoid, and his house had been smashed up in persecution.

It would therefore appear that EAB money was pooled monthly and each missionary family received a fixed percentage. The remainder was distributed to the different needs of the work. Clearly the fixed percentage was very little and they were all finding it hard to survive - hence the bickering. Frank therefore wrote, *"I appeal to you brethren to devise some system of receiving designated monies and sending them as such. All three of us are agreed on this. We would like to suggest designated monies should be given separately and the general fund to be divided according to the size of the family"*.

This debate came out into the open when, in 1956, Albert Mundy was back in Brazil and the three brothers who had made these proposals were on furlough in the UK. Gordon Emmens made a statement in the GTB News No.7 of 23rd June 1956, saying that when he returned to Brazil he would work in a different area and have his own representative and treasurer, and the following edition of GTB News announced this representative and treasurer as E. R. Parnell of Shirley, Southampton. In effect Gordon Emmens and family had therefore ended their service with EAB and were to follow other pathways of service. We know they served God for many years after this in Portugal, and today live in the U.S.A.

Then in edition No. 9, dated December 1956, the GTB News announced exactly what had been requested a couple of years earlier. EAB adopted a policy of designated gifts to missionaries whilst also maintaining a general fund. It was a good decision. Eddie Irish was to handle designated gifts from now, on and Elgie Bergersen would continue handling the general fund. I have no way of being sure, but I suspect that Albert Mundy was also in favour of this change, but the Home Committee treasurer was not. Within less than a year E. Bergersen resigned as EAB treasurer. However, I honestly think that this was a good solution that EAB came up with for tackling a problem which could have wrecked the work. So, as I said at the beginning of this section, problems are inevitable in the work of God, but if we handle them as Christians, and seek God's will, then problems can be stepping stones to growth. This was what happened to EAB. We are not perfect, and we have our ups and downs, but, with all honesty we have laid out this turbulent part of our history, and praise God that He brought us through to a better clearer pathway. We learnt by our mistakes.

Before closing this section I should add that today EAB has become a much more complex Mission and Charity, but supporters may still designate their gifts to support whatever part of the work they so desire and feel on their hearts to support. There is also still a general fund which is distributed to the principal needs of the moment, and general running costs of the Mission. Today all new missionaries, once accepted by the Brazilian and UK Leadership Boards, become associate short-term or long-term missionaries who are entirely responsible for the raising of their own support which is channelled to them through EAB. In this way the door is wide-open for appropriate capable Spirit-filled missionaries in EAB today, whilst avoiding any danger of over loading the central on-going support capacity of EAB as happened years ago.

15. The Patos Building commences

The 1957 New Year saw Albert Mundy and team getting started digging the foundations for the new EAB church in Patos, and bringing in huge boulders of rock to form a solid base for the church 60 feet long and 26 feet wide. By March they had laid 20,000 bricks, but then EAB ran out of money and had to put the work on hold.

Personal letters from both Albert and Daisy Mundy show how much they were looking forward to Frank Dyer's return to Brazil, and the Dyer family's farewell service was set for 24th August in conjunction with EAB's 19th anniversary services both afternoon and evening that day. A week later, on the last day of August, they were bid farewell by a good singing crowd as they boarded the H.M.S. Alcantara, and they docked in Recife on 12th September to be met by Albert, Daisy and Graham Mundy, now a teenager. Elizabeth Dyer once again had the good fortune to have her birthday on board ship during the voyage, so she arrived back aged eight, her brother Sam was six, her other brother David was three and toddler Eunice was two. It was a sleepy but happy and united bunch that headed back to Patos the following morning at 4.30 a.m. They travelled all day on the *"hot, dusty, bumpy road to Patos"*, but by night they were home, and they rented a little terraced bungalow near the Mundys.

Albert and Mary Peasley announced that they were delaying their return to Brazil to the following year, as their daughter was undergoing a series of surgical interventions and had spent seven weeks in Odstock Hospital near Salisbury. However, by the April 1958 edition of GTB News Hazel had been released after five months in hospital and was declared fit enough to return to Brazil with her parents, brother Ian and new born sister Gillian. The old faithful H.M.S. Alcantara was to end its sailing days that month, so the Peasleys were obliged to sail from Liverpool on 19th June, on the ship H.M.S. Hilary, which carried 231 passengers but only sailed as far as Belém, at the mouth of the Amazon in north Brazil, and from there flew to Campina Grande, before travelling the last part of the journey by road to Patos. That evening the Dyers and Peasleys all had tea at the Mundys, and listened to a recording of the farewell service which the Peasleys had brought with them. However such calm would not last for long!

16. Intense Persecution

Looking through Frank Dyer's diary for 1958 everything initially started just as peacefully as the welcome back tea party at the Mundys' house. Evangelist Zacarias Salvador had moved to Coremas on 10th April to lead the young EAB church there, and visits to Coremas and then Misericordia by Albert Mundy and Manoel Lourenço were reported as really blessed of God. However, Albert Mundy was back in Patos with Frank when the first signs of an outrageous period of Catholic persecution broke out in Patos on 21st April. It was to be the start of the worst, longest and most concentrated period of persecution that an EAB church had ever gone through.

Albert Mundy, writing on 3rd April 1958, commented about how the priest, Manoel Dutra, was *"going almost crazy"* with anger at the growth of the evangelicals in Patos, and had christened him *"Friar Lobster"* (referring to Brother Mundy's red sun burnt skin in the tropical heat). Albert said he was calling Frank *"Friar Lizard"* and another brother in the church *"Friar Baldhead"*. *"It is he who needs his head seeing to"*, Brother Mundy reacted, with his normal sense of humour. Then he continued:

"Priest Manoel Dutra went along to one of our Christian's homes the day before yesterday and prohibited her from having services in her home! My word she gave him about the toughest time he has ever had! However he left promising to order the people to stone us and cover us with dirt and ashes, so we are expecting some lively times in the near future"!

Why exactly the explosion of hatred, ignorance, and prejudice occurred in 1958 is probably a combination of various factors. There were only four evangelical churches in the town. The Baptists and EAB arrived in the same year of 1948, and the Congregationals and Presbyterians some years earlier; so it wasn't that there had been a recent influx of churches established in Patos forcing the Catholics to panic. The four churches were going well and were strong churches in the Faith, but there was far from rampant church growth in Patos, so that wasn't the spark that set the bomb off. It was rather the influence of two fanatical Roman Catholic leaders, who irresponsibly whipped up the Catholic faithful into a type of "holy war" spirit against the *"dangerous protestant teachers of a new law"*! For a long time the EAB church members had become used to being humiliated by having maize thrown at them *"to feed the goats"* (as opposed to the Catholic sheep), but now two fanatical leaders came together in Patos and they were willing to go much further and stop at nothing to wipe out the infidels!

The Catholic leadership had just built a new church, not far from the EAB church, called Santo Antonio, in a deliberate effort to check evangelical growth on that side of town. The priest placed in charge of it was called Manoel Dutra. He, in turn, called up reinforcements for the "holy war" in the person of an Italian Friar, called Damião, who had been long known for his radical anti-protestant campaigns of persecution. Here then were two men who were willing to go to any lengths to defeat, whom they saw as the enemies of God, and their aim clearly was to manipulate the simple masses to do their dirty work for them, in the form of mob terror and intimidation. Patos, in 1958, witnessed one of the worst examples of exactly how those who called themselves "Roman Catholic Christians" should never behave. It was not that 1958 was the only example of such persecution of evangelicals in Patos and region, because sadly it happened all the time, but that year was by far more intense and prolonged- than average such occurrences. This fact is underlined by the amount of press coverage that it received in both the secular and religious press.

On 21st April 1958 Frank Dyer reported that Priest Manoel Dutra had been to the borough of Mata Burro in Patos, where EAB was seeing a lot of decisions for Christ, taking with him a lot of rough men carrying the image of *"Our Lady of Fátima"*. He deliberately took the image to an elderly lady's house belonging to the EAB church. A young lad from the mob *"boasted to eight year old Elizabeth that he would bring a sack of ashes to tip on her head"*.

The following day the same priest and mob of hooligans went back to harass the dear lady, and nearly broke her door down to petrify her. They then moved on to our church and pelted the building with stones. The following day Albert Mundy lodged a formal complaint with the Chief of Police who sent several officers to maintain order. Nevertheless the priest reappeared the following evening as the Thursday evening youth meeting was nearing its end, and one of the mob hurled a rock weighing a kilo which missed Brother Cesário by a whisker!

There were a few days' lull, but on 2nd May things took a turn for the worse. Frank Dyer relates what happened:

"Albert Mundy and I were leading an open-air service in front of Sister Madalena's house but during the service Priest Manoel Dutra turned up with his mob carrying the image of "Our Lady of Fátima" again, and positioned themselves right in front of us, with the statue above their shoulders, in a real stand-off provocation".

Before continuing I should mention that sister Madalena was quite a primitive wild sort of lady who had been wonderfully converted. However, accustomed to a life out in the wilds she never took to the idea of showers and was convinced the water tank above her would come down on her head. Hence the sister had an extremely strong body odour! Elizabeth Dyer, however, even as a little girl used to win her over and give her showers and clean her up! Nevertheless, going back to Frank's description of the meeting in front of her home, he continued:

"Suddenly the mob started to hurl stones and sand at us all in the service. It was terrible! But we just carried on singing hymn after hymn and refused to let the meeting be halted, which is what they wanted. This went on for a long time, but when they saw that we were not going to be intimidated they then produced a portable loudspeaker to blast us out!

By this time the Baptist pastor had got word of the trouble and came and stood with us in solidarity. Those were days when Christians of all labels stood together. The standoff continued so the police were called, but they didn't turn up till 40 minutes later, and by that time we all had received a pounding without exception. I myself was hit many times, which left me with several painful bruises, and Brother Bert had skin scraped off his face, and Sister Madalena had a nasty cut over her right eye. The priest shouted that he would not leave before we left but we refused to move not to give him the taste of victory in his mouth. Eventually the police asked us to withdraw, so we did to show our respect for law and authority, but the police asked us to report to the police station the next morning. It was 10.30 p.m. when we left so we went with Baptist Pastor Silas and brethren from there to spend an hour united in prayer.

When we went to the Police Station the next day the leaders of the four evangelical churches in town went together. The Chief of Police was not helpful at all and just ordered us to stay away from Roman Catholic meetings and for the priest to stay away from ours, and call the police in the event of trouble!"

So day by day the trouble grew and the EAB missionaries appealed to the regional chief of police for protection as the local one was clearly in collusion with the priest. They had heard that the next stage was to attack the EAB church, and beat up the people with clubs, staves and truncheons, but the police got wind of this and were sent in to pre-empt it and guarded the EAB church - much to the surprise of the catholic procession that came past the church that night ready for action. My wife Elizabeth comments that it was widely held in evangelical circles at the time that this "police action" was in fact angelical!

By 6th May 1958, the news of the growingly intense persecution reached the state-wide press in the Paraíba Post (Correio da Paraíba) when José Saldanha, a non-evangelical journalist, had the courage to tell the world what was happening in Patos:

"During the evening of 2nd May the city of Patos was the scene of the most lamentable act of religious intolerance. The fanatical crowd, spurred on by a religious guide... committed acts of criminal violence thus flouting both divine and civil law... In the

face of such an unhappy event in the third largest town of our glorious Paraíba... we feel very much ashamed... and responsibility for this act of vandalism must rest squarely on the shoulders of Priest Manoel Dutra who has for some months made threats over a public-address system and led processions right to the doors of Evangelical churches while their meetings were being held. Where is Father Dutra going to stop? Is it possible that he does not understand that the Christian's battle is in the field of thought and persuasion and not in the field of violence and disrespect"?

The troubles continued however and whilst on the one hand meetings were organized by the police authorities to give some sort of impression of a desire to maintain or restore order, on the other hand the same violence continued. Thus Frank Dyer reported on 10th May 1958:

"We were stoned again at our place of worship tonight. As I was closing the doors the catholic procession that was returning from a round the town tour of nuisance, spotted me and put me under a hail of stones, and one nearly broke my thumb".

So things continued night after night in Patos during the month of May, which the Catholics call the "month of Mary". Then on 18th May news reached EAB's headquarters that similar trouble had broken out in Itaporanga when the brethren there came under a shower of stones at the Friday evening prayer meeting! On the 20th Frank Dyer was down with flu, but Ivy went to church and reported that a stone was thrown from the nightly catholic procession and it narrowly missed a baby in the church which would have killed it for certain had it hit. Then on 22nd May Priest Manoel Dutra announced that Friar Damião was coming as a sure reinforcement for his campaign of terror. However, for some reason, he came and went within just a few hours on that occasion. Why this happened we do not know, but he was to return, unfortunately, with his oratory well known in the whole region to incite the Catholics against the Protestants. The catholic masses revered Friar Damião so a very dangerous and ominous combination was forming on the horizon. Friar Damião and Priest

Manoel Dutra were expert mass manipulators and bigger trouble was ahead for sure.

Skirmishes continued throughout that month of May, but the EAB leaders did their best to do nothing that could be interpreted as retaliation or provocation. They realized there was little chance of getting any justice out of the authorities so just left things with the Lord in prayer. However on 4th June Priest Manoel Dutra, using the enormous sway he had with the people, or at least using the authority he thought he had, went to Francisco Oliveira's house and ordered his pregnant wife to no longer allow our services at their house or else he would "knock the house down and hit her head with stones"! This sister was not somebody to mince her words and rightly told him straight what she thought of him. Lo and behold, the priest then reported her for *"insulting a religious authority"* and she was called to attention by the Police Chief!

On 8th June Friar Damião was back and his inflammatory speeches on the loudspeaker system of the Santo Antonio church gathered 10,000 people. That night Frank Dyer reports:

"At 2.15 a.m. we were awakened by an enormous crowd running with flaming torches, singing and shouting. One of them gave a tremendously loud bang on our door which really frightened Ivy, Elizabeth and Samuel. Such acts of intimidation and terror were a continuous reality for us".

On 14th June there was a shoot-out in front of the Baptist church, but as nobody was shot nothing came of it. It certainly was part of the war of nerves orchestrated by Priest Manoel Dutra and Friar Damião. Such was the explosive nature of the situation, with nobody knowing what was going to happen next or how things were going to end up, that a Senator, Ruy Carneiro, came to get a feel of the situation in Patos. The Senator interviewed Albert Mundy and Frank Dyer (EAB), Pastor Silas Melo (Baptist), Pastor Djalma (Congregational) and Pastor Jônatas Barros (Presbyterian) who all told him the whole truth about the dangerous situation in Patos, and he promised to write to the Catholic bishop responsible for the region, but little good that did. Friar Damião had conveniently gone elsewhere for a few days, but on 27th June we heard he was back to make things even worse.

The story is now taken up in an article by Euclides Cavalcante Macedo in a 1997 edition of the Presbyterian Newspaper "Brasil Presbiteriano". He writes:

"Friar Damião, far from being a saint as the Roman Catholic Church now wants to make him, after his death in 1997, was an implacable persecutor of evangelicals, an intolerant terrorist and commander-in-chief of a fanatical militia. Thus on 27th June, 1958, Priest Manoel Dutra went with a mob to order the loudspeaker, playing evangelical music from the top of the church, to be turned off immediately as it was interfering with the visit of Friar Damião. They should only turn it on again once the Friar had left town! The brother responsible for the equipment turned it off and then went straight to lodge a complaint with the Chief of Police. He immediately authorized the continuation of the playing of evangelical music by the Presbyterians, as was their custom. When the Priest heard the music playing again he was furious and rushed to the church with his mob to rip down the sound equipment but was horrified to see Captain Severino, Chief of the Police, waiting there for him and ordering him to return to his own church!

The following day, Eve of Saint Peter's Day, Captain Severino was sacked! This outrageous irresponsible decision gave the green light to the fanatics that they wanted and Friar Damião and Priest Manoel Dutra had effectively taken over Patos! The evangelicals were left without any security at all and there was tension everywhere as to what would happen that night. The evangelical did what they always did – they prayed. The Catholics did what they always did – they schemed.

Remember that it was St. Peter's night – bonfire and firework night all over the north-east of Brazil. Then at 10 p.m. came the ominous announcement on the Santo Antonio Church public address system as a multitude gathered to hear Friar Damião at the midnight mass : 'Not even a trace of Protestants will remain in this town'. Then Friar Damião came to the microphone and wept".

"Friar Damião did not weep with repentance of sadness at all the cruelty practiced by the hordes of fanatics manipulated by himself and Priest Manoel Dutra up to that date", reported the Paraîba Post a few days later. (Correio da Paraíba, 12th July 1958, page 5) *"He wept because as yet he had not achieved his objective. Then the crying Friar Damião spoke to the enormous crowd gathered:*

'Never before have I been demoralized in this way. The first time I am being demoralized is in this catholic town of Patos where the catholic families form an absolute majority but are insulted and provoked by the protestants and by Captain Severino Dias who insulted the Catholic Church. I do not know if I will be able to bear such a blow to my holy ministry'

Friar Damião slowly sat down as if he was collapsing. Then Priest Manoel Dutra came to the microphone to continue with the theatre:

'Do you see my brothers how the holy Friar weeps? (The crowd was incensed, electrified and revolted) He weeps at the demoralization by the Protestants and the insults of the regional police chief. How can we put up with such humiliation? If Friar Damião succumbs to this terrible blow the Catholics of Patos will be guilty if he dies! This in unthinkable! We cannot risk such a disaster. Catholic families must react to save the honour of the Church"!

"With that", Euclides Cavalcante Macedo takes up the story again, *"The crowd turned into an uncontrollable rage and descended in direction of the nearest Evangelical Church, the Presbyterian Church, to destroy it! They ripped out the doors and windows, made an enormous bonfire of the pews and pulpit, shouting and chanting as they did it with great jubilation and letting off hundreds of fireworks in the process. There was nothing the brethren could do. There was no one but God to turn to, and the church was gutted leaving only the outer walls".* The Friar and

Priest remained back at St. Antonio's Church no longer weeping or performing.

Albert Mundy and Frank Dyer heard the enormous commotion, saw the flames, and soon realized what was happening. They knew that from the Presbyterian church they would probably go to the Baptist church next and then to the EAB church on the way back to the "holy mass" with Friar Damião. Thus they rushed down to our church to salvage what they could in the event of our church facing the same onslaught. They took home the piano accordion and the loud-speaker equipment as word came that the mob had moved on and was on its way! Then they prayed as never before in their lives.

The wild mob then ran to the Baptist Church, which was next en route, smashed down the doors and started to pile up the pews to start the next bonfire when suddenly something unexpected happened. Somebody fired six shots from a revolver aimed at the pastor watching the attack from the next door manse amidst all the fireworks and chaos, and bullets hit three people, but killed nobody. To this day no one knows who fired the shots, but it served to disperse the mob who suddenly realized that at any moment they too could be shot. As everyone withdrew to a distance the Mayor, José Cavalcante, and the police arrived at the scene and the crowd quickly cleared off. It would appear that police (or angels?) were sent to guard our church too in the process, so the mob went back to hear Friar Damião at the mass.

The following day threats upon the lives of the EAB leaders and members and the other evangelical pastors, were a constant, and the evangelical leadership were involved in meetings all the time over the coming days as the authorities woke up to the seriousness of the situation; and the press was now telling the story throughout Brazil. Written on the walls of the burnt down Presbyterian church were found the following:

"Get out Goats!.. The biggest bonfire was this church!.. Our deepest sympathies on the death of the Presbyterian Church... Hail

Mary! The Presbyterian church died this Saturday killed by the Catholic Church"!

However there was one distracting factor on that St. Peter's Day that followed the awful burning down of one church, and the planned burning down of the others, which certainly contributed to the violent mob not continuing their destructive rampage as planned. It was the final of the World Cup in Sweden, and Brazil beat Sweden 5 x 2 to win this FIFA trophy for the first of five times so far. So we can say with all honesty that Pelé, Garrincha, Zagalo and team mates indirectly contributed to the survival of EAB that day. Had they lost, there is no knowing what may have happened, but they won, and the Brazilian devotion to football proved stronger than that given by the religious fanatics to persecution. Pelé and Garrincha held more sway than Damião and Dutra! Praise God!

Unbelievably the Roman Catholic Church contracted lawyers to sue us for the responsibility of all that happened! The Brazilian Evangelical Alliance flew envoys from Recife in support of us and advised us to contract lawyers to fight the ridiculous case, which is what we did together as evangelicals from the four churches. A military leader was brought in to try and restore order in Patos.

We know that at some point in all this bedlam a Canadian missionary, called Dennis Pape, was travelling through Patos and soon realized the grave situation facing the evangelicals. He worked with the Inter-Varsity Fellowship (A.B.U) and was on his way to Recife, so he went to the British Consulate there to report the serious danger in which British missionaries found themselves in Patos with constant death threats. Elizabeth Medcraft, née Dyer, who was then eight years old, and present throughout all this uproar, tells us that the Consulate informed the Brazilian Government of their concerns and this triggered an official reaction which helped combat the Catholic mob rule, but we have no way of knowing for sure if this was what brought in a military intervention at this point.

The Brazilian Evangelical Alliance's delegation landed on the Patos dusty airstrip on 1st July 1958, having sent a telegram to the Governor of the State of Paraíba the previous day, as follows:

"Governor Dr. Pedro Gondim. João Pessoa, Paraíba. The Brazilian Evangelical Alliance laments the fanatical religious occurrences provoked by Friar Damião and the local vicar which resulted in the burning and damaging of evangelical churches in Patos, Paraíba. We respectfully request urgent and effective measures to restore the constitutional rights of all citizens in that town. Signed: Rev. Oton Guanais Dourado (Chairman), Torquato Marques dos Santos (Secretary)".

One of the Evangelical Alliance delegation members, Torquato Santos, was a Rotarian and ex-president of Rotary in Recife, so nothing better than to seek out the Patos Rotary president who also turned out to be a lawyer and town council authority, as well as being a Roman Catholic. The Patos Rotary President received the delegation very well, and with him they first visited the Town Hall. It should be said at this point that far from all the Catholics condoned what was going on in Patos and many were ashamed..

From there they visited the main priest in Patos by the name of Sitônio, who called in Priest Assis to aid him, and they gave a long winded explanation of the recent events. Having heard the civil and catholic authorities, the delegation had lunch, and in the afternoon met with all the evangelical leadership of Patos. At this meeting were Pastor Jônatas Barros (Presbyterian), Pastor Silas Melo (Batista), Pastor Djalma Araújo (Congregational), Pastor Albert Mundy (EAB), Pastor Frank Dyer (EAB), and other principal leaders from the four evangelical churches in Patos. In this meeting it was unanimously made clear to the Evangelical Alliance that in no way could the catholic explanation of events be accepted. This explanation, heard in the morning by the delegation, was that things had happened owing to a random group's actions after provocation and had nothing to do with the catholic leadership! All four churches' independent witness was that this had been an orchestrated long term plan of action directed by Priest Manoel Dutra and Friar Damião, who directly manipulated the catholic masses to their own ends. Thus the Evangelical Alliance's final statement said:

"If the higher Ecclesiastical Authorities were incapable of halting the persecution, or of controlling the sadistic manifestation of religious fanaticism, then the State must surround with special precautions Priest Manoel Dutra and Friar Damião so as to guarantee the constitutional rights of all Brazilians".

The secular press carried articles constantly in July and August about the terrible persecution in Patos, and this clearly brought pressure on the Catholics to not repeat their actions, as the world would know. Sadly, however, leading Priest Francisco Sitônio started publishing articles in the Paraíba Post in defence of his colleagues. He argued, in the 20th July edition, that whilst he accepted that religious freedom was part of the Brazilian constitution, it had to be remembered that the Catholics formed the vast majority and that Protestantism is an extremely false religion. Therefore *"it is the natural right not to admit the existence of what is wrong".* In the same newspaper of 26th July Priest Sitônio went on to say that what happened in Patos at the end of June *"could not have been avoided by any member of the catholic clergy".*

Whilst the war of words continued in the press the violence continued in Patos, though somewhat more sporadically. On 16th July Frank Dyer led the open-air service in the borough of Mata Burro (Liberdade) and during the service a Catholic procession came by with the same statue as ever and the same priest as ever. Only 20 yards after passing the EAB service they slowed right down and started chanting *"Long Live the Virgin",* and then somebody hurled a large stone with great force which made a direct hit on Sister Francisca's mother so she had to be rushed to hospital.

This again stirred up the authorities, but at least they were quicker to react this time. Firmino da Silva, an ex-State Deputy and evangelical, came to Patos with the State Governor, Pedro Gondim, and Frank Dyer was involved in meetings with these authorities, and so were the Catholic clergy. It was always the same however, with the inference of the discussions being totally prejudiced, and the Evangelicals were always presumed guilty just for being Evangelicals and a minority. Nevertheless, things were very slowly getting more awkward for the Catholic fanatics, and the Evangelicals held their nerve very well and never reacted at all to intense, prolonged, unprovoked and violent provocation.

The EAB UK Committee was, of course, aware of the goings on in Patos as it received reports and personal letters throughout the period, but these could never convey the full terror of that terrible year of 1958 in which, had it not been for God's protection and mercy, EAB could have lost its two main missionary families and the church in Patos. This was EAB's 20th year, and what a year it had proved to be! Thus on 6th September 1958 two annual meetings were held at 3.15 and 7 p.m. to celebrate God's goodness, and EAB's 20th anniversary, at which Bernard Snelgrove was one of the speakers. In Brazil, the missionaries thought of the meetings that day and were present in Spirit. By God's grace they were still alive to tell the story and continue the difficult battle in Brazil's north-eastern interior against endemic physical and spiritual drought. EAB stuck at the task and never even thought of backing off or running from the battle front. As a consequence, the truth has marched on, and the advocates of religious ignorance and darkness were forced to realize that God is greater than any of man's individual or institutional scheming.

Still today, religious prejudice exists in Patos and region, but is far more timid and covert than 50 years ago. The burnt down Presbyterian Church was rebuilt and expanded, the EAB Church changed location and a much larger one was built, the Baptist church recovered and expanded and the Congregational church has grown too. Added to these four churches that endured the 1958 persecution, have come many other denominations as Patos has grown to have a 100,000 population, and parallel to this a growing evangelical presence. The shots fired in 1958 aimed at the evangelical leadership were, in fact, shots in the feet of the radical Catholic fundamentalist fanatics themselves, and the stones thrown at the believers have been symbolically used to build churches all over Patos for God's glory.

The Evangelicals never retaliated in that awful year; the wheels of God's justice may grind slowly, but they do grind! So it was that the following year, on one Saturday afternoon when fortunately nobody was around or inside, the St. Antonio church (which was the pivotal church of the entire 1958 uprising) saw its roof crash down with no obvious explanation. The roof was rebuilt and reinforced with steel trusses. However, in January 1961 an enormous wind brought the roof down again.

On 17th April 1964 the Evangelical Churches of Patos finally saw the Court case, started by the Catholic Church, come to its conclusion. The Protestants won the case, exactly four days before the sixth anniversary of when all the troubles started, and the State was obliged to pay the churches for the damage caused by the riots of 1958. It wasn't the amount of money that was received that was important. The great importance was that the Brazilian judicial system recognized the total innocence of the evangelicals in the riots and, in the light of the impossibility of pinning the blame on Catholic individuals or the Catholic institution, judged the State guilty of not protecting the Protestants' civil liberties and rights.

In March 2004 I was invited to take part in a live radio programme on the Radio Espinharas which belongs to the Roman Catholic Church. During the programme Priest Luciano finally publicly apologised for 1958 and asked for forgiveness.

17. EAB Consolidates its Headquarters

In early 1959 Albert Mundy was virtually evicted from his rented house in Patos despite having lived there for eight years. Albert was pretty sure this was still the backlash from the 1958 riots, as the Catholic house owners now sought to do their part in making life discreetly difficult for the missionaries. This was no whim of Albert's imagination as this sort of thing still happens up to the present day. Albert had to raise funds to buy land and then build a house, as the Peasleys had already done in Conceição and later the Dyers had to do in Patos. Elizabeth and I were forced to move as many times as the first 12 years we spent in Patos until us too, by God's grace, were given the stability of our own house. This too has been the case as EAB has sought to establish works in different towns and villages, and the only way to survive has been to buy land and build both church and manse.

In April 1959 the EAB fleet of Jeeps became a reality with Frank able to buy a 1942 American military jeep at Princesa Isabel for £300, and a week later Albert Mundy bought a 1951 jeep at Juru. The missionaries stopped to distribute Gospel literature at Juru, and then at Água Branca and Imaculada on the way back. At last they had the transportation independence which was to greatly help the expansion of the Kingdom. Frank, later that year, was thrilled to announce that he had loaded the jeep with the whole family, plus two sisters with their babies, plus hammocks, clothes and loudspeaker equipment, to go and minister at Coremas, and they had covered the 55 mile journey in three hours! (It's just as well they didn't have radar in those days!) Large crowds gathered for the services and they baptized five. Albert Mundy had gone on a similar trip to Itaporanga with a similar load.

The Peasleys reported progress in the work in 1959, but Albert Peasley complained of pain still in both ankles since he broke them both when he fell off the roof when building his house at Conceição. However all the missionaries were reporting, as they travelled to a variety of churches and church plants around the field, that whilst there was progress through decisions for Christ on one hand, there was loss everywhere, owing to the droughts which forced people to move away to survive and find work. This has always been one of the great frustrations for EAB, and one of the major problems in establishing indigenous national strong churches in the interior of north-eastern Brazil. Drought leads to hunger, thirst, unemployment and poverty, and the church members join the regional exodus to survive. This causes two major problems. Firstly, the obvious depletion or complete disintegration of the local church and secondly, the worsening of urban problems in the south, where those that go there from the north-east form vast slum areas vulnerable to every social problem imaginable.

Two issues of considerable importance are evident in the first GTB News of 1960. First of all, Albert and Mary Peasley, with their three children, had effectively left EAB after about one and a half years back in Brazil following their first furlough. Their address was given as a post box in João Pessoa, the capital of Paraíba State on the coast, 190 miles east of Patos, but no other explanation was given. From then on we notice that Albert Peasley never again wrote in any issue of the GTB News, but his wife did make some brief appearances with words of thanks for gifts and general messages that their ministry was going well without specifying exactly how or where. A later edition of GTB News made it clear that the Peasleys had left EAB to work with an American Mission, and that only money specifically designated to the Peasleys was being passed on to them. In 1961 their address was given in Recife, Pernambuco State, but that in November Mary and the children returned to the UK, and in early 1962 all links with the Peasleys were ended with the announcement that from then on all gifts and communications should me made exclusively with their address in Staffordshire. I had fellowship with the Peasleys on a furlough in the 1970s, and I know that in that decade and the following one Albert did attempt a rapprochement with EAB, but it was not to be.

The second important issue which arose immediately at the start of the 1960s, was the possibility of Frank Dyer and family moving to the new capital of Brazil, Brasília, to structure churches that were starting to appear as possibilities owing to people from our churches in the north-east going there for work. It materialised that the visionary Albert Mundy had already visited the brethren there once, and now the May 1960 edition of GTB News was being typed in Brasília where Frank and Albert were together spying out the land and visiting EAB members!

Up until 21st April 1960, the capital of Brazil had been Rio de Janeiro, but the ambitious and courageous project, which some thought crazy, was to build a new purpose-built capital in the heart of the central-western area of Brazil so as to attract and promote the development of vast areas of this part of Brazil; thus exploiting the full potential of the land of this gigantic nation. So Brasília was created from scratch, and the idea of development worked as satellite towns started erupting overnight in the region to provide the workforce for the new capital. Here, indeed, was a brand new mission field previously non-existent, and EAB had the advantage of having quite a number of its members having moved there ahead of even the new capital's inauguration. Frank's declared plan of action was to move to Brasilia's satellite town of Taguatinga and initially establish an EAB church there, but, clearly as the month went by Frank felt unsure if to go or not.

As a fellow visionary, like Albert Mundy, I am writing this nearly 50 years later and shouting out inside me, "Go Frank, Go"! However, I must lay out at this point the pros and cons regarding the venture. The pros were a virgin mission field of Brazilians from the four corners of Brazil, plus a team of members already there, plus the fantastic chance to establish an EAB base at the heart of Brazil where the seat of power was to be, and is to this day, with all the multiple doors that this would open up. The cons were that this was a new world for EAB of urban evangelism, plus this was a very distant place from Patos, so how would the logistics work out? It was also a very expensive place to plant a church and could EAB afford it?

A personal letter from Frank to his prayer partners in September 1960, sums up the dilemma in Frank's heart. He wrote:

"Our jeeps have opened up greater possibilities here, so one naturally feels a little more cautious about moving completely out of the district. Brasília may produce greater results numerically, but what of the scattered villages here with scarcely an opportunity to hear the message of Hope"?

Frank Dyer eventually opted for the scattered villages, as opposed to the strategic move to the Federal Capital, and we have to respect his decision. What would have happened had he have gone we will never know.

In the GTB News of January 1961 Albert Mundy reported eight decisions for Christ in Patos the previous year and 21 in Itaporanga where he mentioned the need for a larger building. He also mentioned his wife's decision to move back to the UK for health reasons, and Daisy flew to England on 27th June 1961.

In March 1961 Frank and Ivy's daughter, Elizabeth, contracted smallpox from which she very nearly died. She was covered from head to toe with spots which turned to blisters and then burst to become infected sores which itched terribly. She even vomited blood. Elizabeth received no medical assistance whatsoever, but her father never left her night and day, and kept sitting her in a bowl of mentholated spirit to ease the itching. The bottoms of her feet were so covered with sores that she could not walk. Miraculously, Elizabeth survived, has the minimum amount of scars from the disease, and is one of the most active leaders in EAB to this day. Praise God! As she was recovering her younger sister, Eunice, caught the same disease, but she gratefully had a much milder version and soon recovered.

Meanwhile, back in the UK Committee there was a change as it was announced that year that Eddie Irish could no longer carry on as the EAB treasurer for health reasons, so Misses P. & J. Mann took on the role of joint honorary treasurers. These sisters, Pearl (to become Skivington) and Joyce (to become Sims), carried on jointly for about a year until Joyce took on the roll alone for nothing less than 25 years!

It must be said at this point how important the international EAB team of missionaries and home committee has always been. EAB has to exist as a team, and the work of all those involved for God's glory over these past more than seventy years are of equal importance in the building of the Kingdom and the expansion of God's work in Brazil. Hundreds, even thousands, have prayed and supported. A variety of brothers and sisters have taken part in the home committee as coordinators, members and treasurers. Many have served as missionaries and as national pastors and evangelists. Others have fulfilled other voluntary roles behind the scenes. However we are all workers together with Christ. We all make up the EAB team past, present and future. To God be the glory!

Towards the end of 1962 new missionaries to work with EAB were announced: Jack & Beth Denton. It so happened that this did not come about as the following year this was announced as cancelled because of Jack's health. Nevertheless, there was an interesting principle established in this case which is fascinating for the current EAB UK Committee and us as directors. The principle was exactly the same as what we call today "Associate Missionaries". For the Dentons were to work with EAB, but were to be entirely responsible for their own financial support. We therefore see the importance of recording and publishing such a history book as this because when we, as directors, agreed this principle with the EAB UK Committee or Board, to come into effect from 1st January 2003, we thought we were innovating! In fact, we were restoring what had been agreed 40 years earlier between a previous committee and previous directors. So too, as we have researched EAB history, we have discovered a variety of principles that we live out in EAB today without having known that we were carrying on in exactly the same vision as held by our founder. This we find very encouraging as in it we surely see the hand of guidance of the Lord.

Thus, for the record, I will now publish the 2003 EAB Associate Missionary document which is also on the EAB website.

"Associate Missionary Status

As from January 1st, 2003, all missionaries other than the executive directors are classified as associate missionaries, as will be, in the future, all long and short term missionary individuals or teams. Therefore any individual or team wishing to work with EAB should kindly read the following prior to applying:–

EAB / ACEV would warmly welcome new workers on short term and long term bases, for specific situations with specific gifts and capacities, as long as they conform to the guidelines agreed by the 2 organisations. However we need to clearly define the process of becoming an EAB Associate Missionary or Associate Missionary Team. As EAB and ACEV work in a unique partnership, it is clearly vital that these two organisations must be respected and consulted, as necessary and appropriate, in the defining and acceptance process of Associate Missionaries, and with reference to their ongoing ministry in Brazil. Any brother or sister in Christ feeling the call of God upon their lives to work with EAB /ACEV in Brazil should follow the following procedure:

1. Approach the EAB committee in writing with appropriate references from their pastor and any other relevant references. Following examination of this documentation the committee would then arrange to interview the candidate. If the committee still felt at least possibly favourable regarding the candidate, then the EAB Directors would be involved in the discussions. (This process could happen in the opposite order, with the EAB Directors being approached first and then the candidate being referred to the EAB Committee.)

2. The EAB Directors would correspond with the candidate, preferably by email.

3. After ample favourable discussion with both the EAB Committee and Directors, the next step would be to consult the ACEV Directorate. If this body was also favourable then initial arrangements would be made, as it was felt appropriate, to receive the candidate, either for a short term visit to Brazil, or for a short term period of service, prior to a possible longer term commitment. Above all else, an eventual ACEV invitation would be vital for the candidate's acceptance to proceed.

4. It must be made clear right from the start that any new candidate to service in Brazil, having had their proposal prayerfully and cautiously considered, would need to raise all the financial support relevant to their period of service in Brazil, for their air fares, and for any other connected expenses, from their own church, family and friends' contacts, without under any circumstances encroaching on existent EAB supporters. The responsibility of financial support is therefore clearly the responsibility, before God, of the candidate.

5. Health insurance is also considered as essential for all new workers coming to Brazil. Long-term missionaries would need to join the Brazilian UNIMED Health Insurance Company immediately upon arrival in Brazil, and short-term missionaries and teams must have travel health insurance before leaving the UK.

6. It must be made clear that all long or short term EAB Associate Missionaries and Missionary Teams must be willing to accept the leadership of the EAB Directors and the ACEV Directorate. The long experience in Brazil of these brothers and sisters in Christ will be of vital importance to the successful development of any ministry with EAB/ACEV in Brazil.

7. EAB will offer all the advice possible in the UK to associate missionaries, and will channel, through its normal routes, all designated gifts to associate missionaries when in Brazil, through their Directors. Associate Missionaries will be able to receive, through EAB, the advantages of tax refunds through Gift Aid etc. EAB will offer space in its regular publications about the work carried out by associate missionaries, subject to the discretion of the EAB Directors and Publications Editor. EAB's Directors will offer full guidance and advice to new Associate Missionaries, especially in their first period of service in Brazil. Such vast experience will prove invaluable to new workers and will be ignored at the Associate Missionary's risk.

8. ACEV will offer the new Associate Missionary, whether long-term or short term, the vital infrastructure and national Brazilian support and space for development of the new worker's ministry for God. ACEV will be looking for well capacitated workers to fill gaps in the expanding work according to the necessity of the hour. Associate Missionaries must be willing to be flexible, adaptable, be prepared to travel, and to grasp a good working knowledge of the Portuguese language. New Associate Missionaries should seek to acquire at least some knowledge of Portuguese prior to arrival in Brazil, but further language teaching will be arranged for new arrivals, though this will have to be paid for by the pupil in question.

9. Any EAB Associate Missionary or Associate Missionary Team would have to be willing to abide by ACEV's rules, teachings and practices. For example:

* It would not be appropriate to consume alcoholic beverages publicly as an evangelical Christian in Brazil.* Short-term Missionary Team members would not be expected to get involved in any form of physical involvement with the opposite sex.

* ACEV's doctrinal position is pluralistic and happy with a variety of Biblical interpretations on some controversial issues. ACEV believes in the beauty of the complex variety of harmony, so any dogmatic attitudes sowing discord amongst the brethren would not be helpful.

10. Any other matters that arise which are not dealt with in this memorandum will be dealt with by the EAB Committee and Directors and by the ACEV Directorate".

Early in 1962 Ivy Dyer had gall bladder surgery in Patos, having suffered a lot of pain during the previous year. Of course, such surgery was still no simple matter in those days, but she recovered well. However another lesson is learnt from this incident, because on a number of occasions we read in the EAB archives how Frank

Dyer made appeals for funding for his wife's operation during 1961, and had to keep postponing it until they had the money. This is why today EAB insists upon their missionaries paying monthly health insurance, because such delays can sometimes be very detrimental to their health and sometimes health problems arise which just cannot wait, or, are of a colossal cost which nobody can afford.

An important educational initiative was commenced in Patos by EAB in 1962 with the launching of the Mission's first school. The "Eduardo Mundy Primary School" was founded in partnership with the Town Council on 6th October 1962, when Otávio Pires de Lacerda was Mayor. The school had 180 pupils and four teachers. Three of these were funded by the Council and one by EAB. Another school was started in this period, up in the mountains in the Serra Grande region. That year the EAB anniversary in Southampton had Pastor Ivor Thomas, from the Portsmouth Elim Church as the main speaker, and Frank Dyer's sisters, Gwen aged 42 and Rosemary aged 33, gave an account of their visit earlier that year to Brazil.

The inauguration of EAB's first school

Albert Mundy made it quite clear that he wished to be in the UK for the 25th anniversary of EAB for what he intended to be a short furlough. His passport shows us that he left with Graham on 12th June 1963, so as to arrive in the UK in good time for the EAB anniversary meetings on August 24th. Albert and Graham flew "to London Airport by Comet". Prior to leaving, however, EAB managed to gather enough funds and sort out the complete registration of the land, so as to be able to complete the building of the EAB Patos church and inaugurate it on 12th May.

The problem of the legal registration of the land is a classic example of Roman Catholic bias in Brazil. For most of the land in Brazil is freehold property of the Roman Catholic Church, even though private purchasing of long-term leasing was normal and the Catholics just collected the freehold rent. However, this gave the Catholics the power to block the sale of land to Protestants and this they certainly did. The way EAB got round this outrageous situation was for an individual to buy the land and then pass it on to EAB. However, if the Catholic authorities became aware of this they would still block the sale. This happened in Patos and it took a lot of negotiation and pressure to finally release the land to the Mission for legal registration.

This having been achieved, the final stage of the building work got under way at the start of 1963, and in the GTB News of February Albert made an appeal for funds to help complete the building: *"If you would like to help in this matter, maybe somebody would like to put a window in. This would cost about £15 and there are twelve such"*. My wife, Elizabeth, clearly remembers how many supporters did contribute in this way and thus enabled EAB to complete the construction of this strategic church. Thus 12th May 1963 was another landmark in EAB history as we moved out of a cramped meeting hall, in the same street, and into a large church on the corner of Prado Street and Dom Pedro II Street. Only the baptistery, vestry and first floor Sunday school room, initially built for the choir, was not built for the inauguration, but the main building was completely finished.

**The inauguration service of the EAB Patos church in 1963
being led by Albert Mundy**

Thus Albert Mundy arrived at EAB's 25th anniversary services, held at the Southampton Elim Church which was exactly the same place his farewell service had been held at in 1938. However, the building was a new one as the old one was bombed in the war. Millbrook Road Pentecostal Church provided the tea between the afternoon and evening services, and Albert and Daisy cut a huge commemorative cake which had written on it, "Praise the Lord for 25 Years"! At the services Albert Mundy distributed the following 25th anniversary report:

"The work of the Mission today comprises of pioneering with the Gospel in the unevangelized parts of Brazil. Countless numbers have been won for Christ over the past 25 years. The focus of the work is in the States of Pernambuco and Paraíba which total 69,188 square miles compared with England's 50,875 square miles.

The work is directed from an inland city called Patos which is in a dry barren area, owing to continual droughts, and means that poverty, ignorance, superstition and suffering reign and the people await liberation.

We now have four well built churches at Princesa Isabel, Patos, and Conceição in Paraíba State, and at Jasmin in Pernambuco State. We also have seven outstations spread over a very large area involving long trying journeys. We run two schools at Patos and Serra Grande, and we carry out famine relief distributing food we receive from the USA's Alliance for Progress Programme of social help for the starving thousands in Latin America as launched by John F. Kennedy. To run all this, apart from the missionaries, we have a very devoted band of consecrated Brazilian workers".

This then was the summary of EAB progress over the first 25 years of its ministry. Years of much sacrifice and hardship as the Mundys lost two children and the Dyers saw two of theirs miraculously survive smallpox. These were also years of thousands of miles of travelling, and contributions to the propagation of the Gospel in the north-eastern interior by various missionaries and national workers. It was also a period in which a growing social awareness became evident within EAB and an incipient integral mission approach became evident. In the February 1963 'GTB News' Albert refers to his son Graham and a national worker having been to Campina Grande to get two large lorry loads of food for the hungry, donated by the USA. This provided three tons of food to be distributed by each of the four evangelical churches in Patos. It was a large task to organize such distribution and fill in all the forms required by the USA. Elizabeth, my wife, then 13 years old, was responsible for the administration of this project at that young age. She also had a Sunday school class of 120 children parallel to this, so on top of her regular schooling she had plenty to do.

Daisy Mundy was returning to Brazil with her husband and son at the end of this furlough and Albert expressed their disappointment at not being able to get a ship back till January 1964, because he had promised the Christians in Brazil to try and be back for the Christmas Conference. He announced, however, that they were booked on a cargo boat for 13th January sailing from Swansea. However, this was postponed to 31st January and eventually was completely cancelled, so frustration mounted. Time passed and it was not until 6th August 1964 that the Mundys sailed from Southampton on the Cunard Liner "The Queen Elizabeth" to New York, and from there on a tramp steamer, S.S. Mormacwren, finally arriving at Recife on 27th October where they were met by Frank Dyer. Albert remarked how happy he was to see Frank as *"we were given to understand that things were very difficult in Brazil".*

The difficulties in Brazil that Brother Mundy referred to was the coup that had taken place on 31st March that year, overthrowing the democratically elected government led by President João Goulart, and bringing in an often brutal military regime for the following 21 years. The military dictatorship swept to power on an anti-communist platform, pursued avidly all that were mildly pink, let alone red, many lost their lives and were tortured, and a general spirit of conspiracy and anti-conspiracy came to dominate the nation. Many spied on their fellow Brazilians and reported them to the regime if they thought they had communist tendencies. It was a dark period in which freedom of expression was increasingly crushed. Censorship was everywhere, so often the newspapers printed cake recipes on their front pages as the only means of protest open to them.

The work of EAB did not suffer as a result of the military rule, but other church groups did, especially the Presbyterian Church, which in Recife saw pastors denouncing even their fellow pastors, as told in a sadly powerful book written by Pastor João Dias de Araújo called "Inquisição sem fogueiras" (Inquisition without bonfires).

Despite the negative side of this period, there was a great nationalistic development drive nationwide and there were good things done. Telecommunications, for example, were modernized and completely transformed in Brazil and road networks were greatly improved. However, in the process, the regime built up an enormous external debt to finance all it did, and it has only been in recent years that this has been tackled and the chronic endemic inflation generated was brought under control.

This is what the Mundys were returning to, so no wonder that Albert was pleased to see Frank walk onto their ship in Recife at 8.30 a.m. that morning in Recife. Frank represented normality and someone he could quietly talk to and find out what was going on. For, in those days, nobody spoke loudly about these matters *"as you never knew who was listening and could report you"!*

However, Albert and Frank were not just concerned about the political unrest in the country. Their social awareness was increasing and Albert was bringing money back from the UK *"to build an orphanage or an old people's home"* and Frank wrote in February 1964 about the need to build a hostel for down and outs, who once helped could be "helped to find work". They certainly had plenty of time to discuss all these matters as they were stuck for two weeks getting the Mundys' baggage released from customs. They had brought an electric guitar for Graham, a tape recorder and a record player, to mention just a few items which came partially from England, but also from brothers and sisters in the USA. Thus Albert's plans when he left for furlough on 12th June 1963, *"to be back in Brazil by Christmas"*, missed the target by about a year, as they finally returned to Patos in mid-November 1964, but they received a traditionally warm Brazilian welcome just the same.

In Albert Mundy's absence, Frank Dyer had ably continued in the leadership of the work, and the areas of work laid out at the 25th annual meetings were amply maintained, as Frank proudly announced how much his daughter, Elizabeth, was able to answer questions posed at the end of meetings by enquirers about the Gospel. Frank added:

"It would have been an encouragement to you all if you could have heard the forthright way that she replied...several signified their desire to follow the Lord at the end, and one of them asked for a

lift afterwards and commented that it had been the first time that he had heard the Gospel".

When I was researching for this book I managed to obtain copies of all the EAB UK Committee meetings from 1964 onwards, so from now on I have them as an added source of information. However, I was naturally frustrated at not having the minutes for the years prior to this and enquired as to their whereabouts. David Shearing, present day UK Board member and son of Pastor Winston Shearing who was the main stay of the UK committee from the start, suggested that there were none *"as things were done so informally in those days".* I honestly could not believe this could be true, but now upon reading the first sets of minutes I think he may be right. My hunch is that a woman joining the committee and with typing skills, Joyce Sims, may have got proper minutes keeping started. In the second set of minutes that I have, dated 28th October 1964, it is recorded that, *"It was agreed that a folder should be purchased in which to keep the typed minutes of the Committee meetings".* It certainly sounds like this was a new idea!

Some interesting details of the first minutes are that, first of all, in the Board meeting of 27th July 1964, Albert Mundy was on furlough and he chaired the meeting and announced that he had invited Clifford Sims, Deryck Scard and Harry Evans to join the committee, and that they had accepted. Thus, on this date present at the meeting were Albert Mundy, Stanley Dibden, Harry Evans, Deryck Scard, Winston Shearing and Clifford Sims. In the following meeting, on 28th October 1964, Joyce Sims, Jack Dyer and Eddie Irish were also present. In this year Elgie Bergersen was in the process of retiring from the committee.

In the GTB News of March 1965 Frank Dyer refers to travelling up into the mountains with Bert, Daisy, Graham and four Brazilians, to minister at at a small farm in Maturéia. He rejoiced at having renewed fellowship with a Christian family there and having preached to some people who had never heard the Gospel before. I preached at this place in 1972, shortly after arriving in Brazil. I remember before the service, (lit by paraffin lamp) being served manioc flour, rolled into a sort of pancake shape, and strong sweet black coffee. It is wonderful to see a fine EAB/ACEV church in the centre of Maturéia today with 86 regular participants, a school at its rear, and two rural church plants, with another 24 regular participants. Praise God!

By 1965 the baptistery, vestry, and upper balcony for the choir, had been built as an extension at the rear of the Patos church, so in the May anniversary service of the Patos church the first baptismal was held in the new baptistery with 18 being baptised! In fact, Albert Mundy commented in July 1965 that *"the work shows progress everywhere"*. Frank Dyer also reports a return to Maturéia, where they held an open-air service in the market in town. The local priest objected and started ringing the church bell so as to drown out the EAB team, but the Chief of Police went and cut the bell rope and solved the problem! The Gospel was also still being preached in Itaporanga, Conceição, Serra Grande and Jasmin in Pernambuco, and souls were being added to the church. Only Princesa Isabel, the original EAB church, was at a standstill.

In 1965 a new work was opened at Teixeira where Frank and Albert had preached for the first time. It was a small town up in the mountains, not far from Maturéia. EAB even rented a house there so as to have a base around which to establish the new work. In June 1965 the Dyers had their fifth child, Esther. It was around this time that Frank, on the way home from preaching at São Mamede a small town 15 miles east of Patos, saw an anteater in the jeep's headlights, and decided to stop and run after it for fun. However, he got more than he had bargained for, and was attacked by the creature which ferociously attacked with its long claws badly tearing Frank's hands and a leg.

Later in 1965, having completed an eight year term of service, it was time for the Dyer family to have a furlough, and Ivy flew to London Airport first, on 6th October, with the three youngest children who were baby Esther, Eunice aged ten, and David aged 11. Frank followed on 6th December with Samuel aged 14, and Elizabeth aged 16, so as to enable them to complete their school years. EAB held a welcome home service for them all on 8th December 1965. Daisy Mundy was again suffering ill health in

Brazil by this time, so she decided to come home on the same flight as Ivy and recover in England.

On 30th January 1966 EAB inaugurated a church building at Itaporanga in which the church still meets to this day. EAB had been ministering here for 20 years, but had always had to manage with rented meeting halls. Now God had made it possible for EAB to build a nice church for the glory of God, and great crowds gathered for its opening. What a change this was for a place that had stoned Albert Mundy two decades earlier, and where Bibles and tracts had been regularly ripped up before them, to taunt them. However, the Christians had stood firm and God had given the victory! EAB was also now reaching to towns like Malta, Condado and Santa Terezinha. Steadily the work of the Mission was gathering pace.

Whilst on furlough in 1966 Frank Dyer was asked to give a brief overview of the work of EAB and this was published in the GTB News of November 1966. In this he said that, 28 years on from its commencement, EAB was still essentially an evangelistic Mission, though running a Primary school and carrying out "relief work". EAB now had five church buildings at Patos, Princesa Isabel, Conceição, Itaporanga and Jasmin, plus nine other towns where small groups of believers meet in rented meeting halls. On top of this the missionaries travelled constantly evangelizing *"hamlets, villages and towns"* all round the region where most still remained hardened to the Gospel.

In the October of 1966 Elizabeth Dyer travelled to Peniel Chapel in London where I was part of the youth. She travelled with the 'Millbrook Christian Centre Southampton' youth, who sometimes organized fellowship visits to hold united services. Peniel Chapel supported missionary work in another part of Brazil to EAB. I had long been enthused about the country since childhood and felt a clear tendency to working for God one day in Brazil. To my surprise and delight Elizabeth, who I had never heard of previously, was invited to sing a solo in the evening service and she sang Psalm 51 in Portuguese which hit me right between the eyes. We met once that winter, in Southampton, where I had gone to take part in a cross country race. The following Easter, her father was invited to speak at my church in London so I asked my friend, David Irish, to convey an invitation to Elizabeth and her brother Sam to have lunch at my house on Good Friday. Thus at Easter 1967, we started going out together, were engaged at Christmas and married in 1969. I do not need to tell anyone which is our favourite Psalm!

It is interesting how God guides people's lives. Elizabeth had gone to England in 1965 to settle there. She met me who felt God's pull in the direction of Brazil. EAB had a home committee leader in Pastor Winston Shearing who was a man of prayer and discernment. He always prayed Elizabeth back to Brazil because of "her commitment to Christ, ability with the Portuguese language, and understanding of Brazilian culture". He also encouraged me, whom he had known from an early age. Thus feeling God's call on my life, and sensing this call confirmed or endorsed by an experienced pastor, I went to the International Bible Training Institute in February 1969 to train for missionary service.

Back in Brazil during 1967 Albert Mundy continued leading the work of EAB as it approached its 30th anniversary. God again was challenging Albert's heart to move further a field with the Gospel as many members had moved south to find work. Thus Albert commenced to establish contacts and make visits to the vast city of São Paulo, about 1,800 miles south of Patos. Parallel to this EAB established a work more fully at Malta, spread in the interior of Paraíba State; preaching at São José de Espinharas; whilst maintaining the churches and church plants already in motion. Sadly in 1967 our leader at Itaporanga, Antônio Ferreira, known as Antônio Pirambeba, lost his wife when giving birth to her 22nd child.

In November 1967 Brother Mundy moved down to São Paulo *"for an indefinite period"* so as to establish the work of EAB there and reported that Evangelist Zacarias Salvador was doing an excellent job in the leadership of the work in the mountains at Teixeira. Conceição was reported as enjoying spiritual progress too. Brother Miguel Serafim was appointed as leader of the work at Malta.

Albert Mundy seems to have really gone to and fro in 1967 to maintain the work in the north-east, whilst flying down to the south-east to establish churches in São Paulo. However, he commented that he was thinking of moving to São Paulo permanently as he could not keep up this constant travelling over such great distances. That year Albert's son Graham married Jandira, (a Presbyterian girl), in the Patos church.

Frank Dyer returned to Brazil in 1968 leaving his wife to care for the family at Dibden Purlieu, on the edge of the New Forest, a few miles from their home church at Hardley Green. Albert Mundy was continuing that year his 1,800 miles each way pilgrimages to São Paulo. He certainly was a man of vision and determination. In a June letter he talks about the church at Mauá, in Greater São Paulo, going well, but needing to buy land so as to build a church and get out of rented halls; which is a challenge which has always faced us and still does. Albert travelled back that month from São Paulo by non-stop coach. I did this when younger, but it was an act of considerable courage for him to do this at 64 years of age.

Another important step forward for EAB occurred in 1968 with the start of a church plant in the large city of Campina Grande, 112 miles east of Patos. Three families moved from Patos to Campina Grande: Antônio Lins de Albuquerque, Terezinha de Lucena Pereira and Ivone Silva Meira and they formed the basis of the new church, which initially met in the Lins' home. They soon moved, however, to a little meeting hall 24 feet long by 15 feet wide on the corner of São Paulo Street and Rio de Janeiro Street in the Liberdade Borough. At the opening of the little EAB hall, Albert Mundy led the service and also present from Patos were Elder Cesário de Paula Conserva; Evangelist Zacarias, (who also visited the work monthly for the monthly communion service); church treasurer Manoel Clementino; Deacon Vicente de Paula Conserva; and Xandu Soares. Campina Grande residents present were the Lins family; with seven members plus their niece called Lusimar da Silva Santos; Terezinha de Lucena Pereira; Ivone Meira and her daughters Ione e Ivonete. Sister Ivone and her daughters are stalwarts in the church to this day. Slowly the EAB church at Campina Grande grew and they moved from rented hall to rented hall, but all were very poor and humble, with not even toilet facilities. Today, this church is the largest EAB church with 205 members plus another 100 participants as well as three branch churches. It has its own large church building as well as Bible College, Action School, and office block. God is faithful.

18. Xandu Soares and Legalism

At some point in this history of EAB we cannot avoid the subject of legalism and of one very strong figure in the first 30 years or so of the Mission, called Xandu Soares. Not that Xandu was the only person responsible for the legalism that developed in the EAB churches, but she was a key maintainer and propagator of it. She, too, became a far too dominant figure within the Mission which we were to eventually regret.

Xandu was the daughter of the first family that the Mundys were welcomed by, back in 1940, at Princesa Isabel, and she soon moved in to live with the Mundys. The positive side of Xandu was that she was a very resolute staunch Christian worker, who was to blaze the trail for many women workers over the decades in EAB. The Mission has never had any difficulty in naturally absorbing women's ministry, and the fact that men and women are "one in Christ" is never questioned in our churches. The negative side of Xandu was that she was an incredibly domineering person, whose shadow towered over nearly all else in EAB. As EAB had never developed an organizational structure to administer such issues, this left her to act as will. That is, no EAB constitution existed until 1973 to distribute responsibilities in the work and there was, therefore, no democratically elected team of leadership as we have today and which has a four year mandate.

Living with the Mundys, Xandu learnt to speak and write English so over the years, as one reads through the EAB newsletters and publications, one finds, quite often, reports from Xandu alongside those of Albert Mundy and Frank Dyer. This was a notable phenomenon because no other Brazilian worker whatsoever had this privilege. Certainly this bilingualism added to her dominant authority, and when this propagated outright legalism we were on a dangerous road.

What I mean by outright legalism is the belief that a list of rules and regulations, as maintained by the Pharisees in Jesus' day, had to be a major factor in controlling the behaviour and appearance of the evangelical Christians, and the following of these rules were the means by which EAB recognized who was or was not a Christian! There were always more rules for women than for men. Thus women could not shave their legs or trim their hair at all. Women had to wear sleeved dresses or blouses and the skirt had to be at least 5 centimetres below the knee. Women could not wear any form of adornment, not even hair clips! Neither men nor women could practice sport, and so the list went on and on. Xandu Soares was a very strong advocate of such legalism and would often publicly humiliate people if they did not comply with the rules. Hence, for example, if a woman went to sing a solo at the front of the church and her skirt was slightly shorter than Xandu ordained, she would go up to the woman and tug her skirt publicly so as to show it was too short.

Ivy Dyer thus tells me that Albert's son, Graham, was not allowed out to play with the local children, but maintained indoors to protect him from contamination from the world. Frank Dyer was more tolerant with his children and allowed them to play table tennis hidden in a back room behind closed doors, or football in a hidden garden. Elizabeth tells me that once Albert discovered Frank was allowing football in this way and told him off! This then was the EAB church regime up till I arrived in Brazil in 1972. My position was always to seek to live according to the Bible and not according to extra-Biblical rules. My position was always to live as a Christian in the same way anywhere, other than in the case of some local cultural issue that needed to be observed. However, to argue that I could not play football in Brazil "for cultural reasons", as was thrown at me in 1972, was the worst joke I had ever heard. After all, Brazil then was already three times world champion, has added two more Cups to the collection by now and where will the list end?

1969 had a very blessed start to the year and Albert Mundy, writing in the March GTB News, described the church in Patos as *"heaven on earth"*. He described journeys also by himself, Frank and national workers, to Itaporanga; Conceição which he said was *"the best visit there ever experienced"*; Jasmin, and Aguiar. He reports a total of 32 conversions in these places in the first quarter of 1969.

Towards the end of the March publication Albert states that, *"three of our young men have set out to study at the Bible School in Recife where they are going to prepare for the work of the Lord. They are willing to sacrifice anything to tell others about the saving and healing power of the Lord Jesus"*. These three men were Elpídio, who led the Campina Grande church for a while in the early days; Edivaldo and Antônio. Unfortunately none of these men were successful at Bible School, their ministries came to nothing and they gave up their courses without completing them. This certainly would not have been helped by the anti-study spirit in EAB churches up to this time. When my wife went to High School in the 1960s she was frowned upon by Xandu and comrades. Imagine then the strain that these three young men would have come under when going to study theology, instead of 'opening your mouth and letting the Holy Spirit fill it' as was the order of the day.

Nevertheless the fact that an attempt was made to train leaders *"for the work of the Lord"* was a step forward and showed that at least some in our churches were becoming aware of this need. This was progress and a landmark for EAB. We came to realize that it would be far better to set up Bible Colleges in the interior, not only because of this unsuccessful experience, but because other denominations too had discovered that students that go to the coast either lose their way or stay at the coast. Hence, in early 1997 EAB started its first Bible College in the interior and today has three, which are really being blessed as instruments in God's hand to train many top class workers and leaders.

On 10th July 1969, Albert Mundy took his son Graham with his wife Jandira and their little daughter Beverley, to England, flying on a TAP (Portuguese Airlines) Boeing 707 via Lisbon–we had come a long way from the slow ships and precarious planes of the past! — They were all at our wedding in November that year.

In England, Albert was full of the blessing in São Paulo and said, *"In the past two years I have spent in all nine months in São Paulo where we have three churches at Mauá, Casa Verde and Itaím Paulista".* These three churches were in Greater São Paulo, but far from the centre. Nevertheless, it was an amazing achievement for EAB to have established these churches in the largest and fast-growing city of São Paulo and, had it not been for that awful word 'legalism', EAB would be a lot stronger for them today. Sadly, however, as EAB later moved further and further away from legalism it proved logistically impossible to share the same vision, always at 1,800 miles apart and eventually we went our separate ways.

In the UK, Albert also reported growth in north-east Brazil at Malta and Condado, and said that people were being converted in the rural area of that region. He also spoke warmly about Teixeira, *"on the top of a big mountain range; a real stronghold of crime and a fanatical R.C. bulwark".* He said that EAB had bought land at Teixeira to build a church in the future, but in the meantime we were using a garage and workshop erected on the land. The garage had been adapted into a meeting hall and the workshop into living quarters for Evangelist Zacarias. From here Zacarias was evangelizing Imaculada, Água Branca and Santa Terezinha over the border in the State of Pernambuco.

19. A Genuine EAB Wedding

In October 1969 Frank Dyer flew back to the UK for the wedding of his eldest daughter Elizabeth to me. I was finishing my year at the IBTI, having been involved in evangelistic campaigns with IBTI in Ireland and Luxembourg. In Luxembourg I had the privilege of being an instrument in God's hands to found a Portuguese-speaking church in the city. I watched the Americans land on the moon in a street café whilst there.

At our wedding there was a flock of pastors. Frank Dyer was there, of course, to give away his daughter, and Colin Whittaker, an Assemblies of God pastor and friend for many years, together with his wife who sang a solo in the ceremony. The wedding itself had four pastors at the front who conducted the ceremony. EAB's UK Committee anchorman from day one, Pastor Winston Shearing, led the service; and alongside him was EAB's founder; Albert Mundy, another EAB Committee member, Pastor Jack Dyer; and Pastor Reuben Gunter from my church of origin, Peniel Chapel. Of course Elizabeth's mother was there together with her brothers and sisters, who were all born in Brazil. Also there were Graham, Jandira and Beverley Mundy from Patos, and other EAB Committee members present were Eddie Irish and Joyce Sims. After our honeymoon we continued our joint preparations for long-term service with EAB in Brazil, with further Bible Study in the USA in 1970 and 1971. Looking back it is good to remember how we were accepted as part of the EAB team (going to Brazil in August 1972), by EAB founder Albert Mundy, EAB Committee original Winston Shearing plus, of course, all the UK Committee.

Frank Dyer found himself torn between two poles of responsibility in 1970 because, even though his eldest daughter was now married, he still had four more children and his wife in the UK. On the other hand he felt his responsibility in Brazil with EAB. For the time being he decided to give priority to the family in England so stayed put. In one Committee meeting Frank's dilemma was expressed and essentially it was said that Frank did not feel a definitely leading from God as to what to do, and upon Albert Mundy being asked what would happen if he was unable to carry on, Albert answered that he believed that "Brother Frank would return in that event". This was indeed exactly what happened when Albert Mundy was killed in a road accident in Brazil the following year. Frank Dyer dropped everything and returned to Brazil immediately to take hold of the reins of EAB.

Another difficult aspect of this period at the beginning of the 1970s was that Pastor Winston Shearing, founder EAB Committee member, was seriously ill with a brain tumour. The first sign that he had any health problem was right in the middle of our wedding ceremony, when he had great difficulty in pronouncing Elizabeth's name. Only sometime later did we come to know that he had a serious problem, and the June 1970 GTB News starts, "With our Secretary, Pastor Winston Shearing, out of active service, our news letters have been difficult to circulate". It was a strange coincidence that the Lord called home both home and overseas EAB anchormen, Winston Shearing, and Albert Mundy, in the following year of 1971. Any Mission goes through problems from time to time, but the early 1970s proved to be the apex of an accumulation of difficulties for EAB. It was indeed a time of great trial and tribulation, and it was exactly in the middle of this period that I was called by God to enter the work in north-east Brazil with EAB. Back in Brazil, Albert Mundy was out of action with illness too,(for the first two months of 1970), but once stronger he recommenced his north-south trips seeking to maintain the north and expand the south in terms of EAB Ministry.

20. The end of an Era but not of EAB

At the end of 1970 Albert Mundy started on yet another of his innovative ideas to expand the work of the Mission for God's glory. He had long dreamed of having a large tent to use as a portable church to expand evangelism and church planting in new towns, villages and communities, and the making of this tent continued until February 1971. How I admire Albert's vision, creativity and disposition. He was quite a character! He wanted to win souls for Christ in a variety of ways and places, using all means available. Thus Albert had *"a band of faithful workers"* making this huge tent by hand and he inaugurated it on Tuesday 23rd February 1971 in Patos, with an attendance of 300 people. Albert ran the inaugural tent campaign for four nights culminating on the Friday, when he anticipated by one day the celebration of the 48th anniversary of his conversion to Christianity. It was a festive occasion and he was thrilled celebrating 48 years following Jesus in the new tent he and his team had made. The next day, 27th February, he was leaving for Recife en route to flying to São Paulo so he warmly shook hands with each brother and sister at the end of that special service that evening. He said, "I am off to São Paulo tomorrow and I don't know if I will return". He did not return.

He travelled all day on Saturday to Recife staying with his Swedish missionary friends for the night. On Sunday morning, 28th February 1971, he called a taxi to take him to Guararapes Airport on the other side of Recife from where he had spent the night. Tragically, for some unknown reason, the taxi driver lost control of the vehicle on the way, and collided with a concrete lamp post on the side of the car where Albert was travelling. Albert received severe head injuries and was rushed to the "Hospital de Pronto Socorro de Recife" (Recife First Aid Hospital) where he was admitted. News only reached the EAB Committee in England two days later concerning the accident, when the British Consulate sent them a cablegram. The cablegram said that Albert Mundy was to undergo surgery and that they would be able to give further information after 72 hours.

Thus the following evening, Wednesday 3rd March, the EAB Committee met in emergency session with the following present: Eddie Irish (Chairman), Stanley Dibden, Frank Dyer, Jack Dyer, Deryck Scard, Clifford Sims, Joyce Sims, Graham Mundy, and Pastor C. J. Charman. Frank informed the committee that his sister Gwen had cabled the Consulate in Recife asking for an update, but had received no reply. It was decided that Frank should phone the "Consulate Department in London" the following morning seeking further information. Frank also started making immediate arrangements to return to Brazil.

That very same evening at 11 p.m. Albert passed into the presence of the Lord. The cause of death on his death certificate is given as "brain haemorrhage caused by cerebral traumatism". Obviously the subsequent autopsy delayed the release of his body and the death certificate was only issued on17th March. This gave time for Frank Dyer to organize his flight to Brazil and he arrived there the day that Albert Mundy's body, having been embalmed, was released for burial in Patos. Graham, Albert's son, also travelled with Frank to be at his father's funeral. The vehicle carrying Albert's body left at a similar time to Frank, but Frank arrived in Patos first because the driver of the funeral company lost the way and was delayed. Meanwhile, the Patos Town Council registered their condolences in a solemn session of the Council concerning Pastor Mundy's death and Councillor Rénio Araújo Torres spoke of the "sadness that the whole evangelical family in Patos would be feeling". Councillor Wilson Dias Novo spoke of Albert Mundy's "great personality" saying that "in Patos his memory would always be reverenced".

When the coffin did finally arrive in Patos, it was good that Pastor Frank Dyer was there already to take care of the proceedings, as there was great commotion and emotion with hundreds gathering to file past Brother Mundy's body. The emotion of the moment led some of the church leaders to seek special authorization from the Town Council for Albert's body to be buried in the EAB church, and this was granted. Frank was not in favour of this, and nor were many others, but the majority wanted this and Frank, only just having returned from a long period away did not feel he was in a position to negotiate anything to the contrary. Thus, Frank Dyer conducted a very emotive funeral service on a hot afternoon, starting at 3.30 p.m. with the church packed beyond capacity and the street outside too. The traffic police blocked off Prado Street for the afternoon so as to allow for the crowds.

The remarkable thing was that the enormous crowd that gathered on that sweltering March afternoon was not made up exclusively of Evangelicals. Mrs. Socorro de Oliveira, who was 27 at the time and was far from being a Christian, but who is a member of our church today, tells me how she managed to squeeze into the church with her mother for the funeral service. Her mother, Maria das Neves, was a renouned school teacher and staunch Catholic to this day, had been invited amongst many other people in authority. *"Priest Laíres even went"*, she pointed out. A leading man from the justice department, Dr. Francisco Torres, also was there, Socorro remembers. Thus the respect that Albert Mundy had earned over the years was reflected on the day he was laid to rest.

Albert's body was laid to rest inside the EAB Patos church at the front, immediately in front of the lower platform. Later a marble plaque was placed on the floor at the head of where the coffin was buried. This remained in place for a number of years, but in agreement with the family this was eventually removed because it was generating visits to the grave at the end of the services, which was not conducive to the on-going life of the church. It was causing a distraction that certainly Albert would never have wanted. Graham, Albert's only son, later discussed the removal of his father's earthly remains to a cemetery, but nobody has ever got round to doing this. Thus today, the younger generation is not even aware of this detail and Albert, joined many years later by his wife Daisy, and are together forever with the Lord.

The EAB Committee met on 30th June 1971, and Ivy Dyer was also present; with Eddie Irish chairing the meeting and Jack Dyer, Joyce Sims, Clifford Sims and Deryck Scard also present. At this meeting Frank Dyer was officially appointed as EAB Field Superintendent or Director, thus replacing the founder Albert Mundy. The minutes state that *"Mr. Frank Dyer is authorized by the Committee to undertake all matters in Brazil on their behalf".* Ivy Dyer informed the Committee that she would be returning to Brazil with her youngest daughter, Esther, within three months. They returned on 8th October 1971.

An obituary for Brother Mundy was published in the Christian Herald of 24th July 1971.

1971 was therefore a year of traumatic change for EAB, and this was not only the case on the field in Brazil because in October 1971 Pastor Winston Shearing also received his homecall from the Lord. Pastor Shearing was a gentle, loving, happy, wise Christian leader, and it was amazing how the original field leader and the original home leader of the Mission were both taken by God to their reward in the same year. It was a testing time for all.

21. Turbulent Times

The EAB UK Committee was informed via Frank Dyer in 1971 that a certain Ralph Moulton, a Baptist minister from the USA, who had supported Albert Mundy in Brazil since 1944 without EAB's knowledge, had expressed a desire to move with his family to Brazil and join the work of EAB. Albert Mundy had met Ralph Moulton in Brazil in the war years when Mr. Moulton visited Brazil with the US navy. There was nothing out of order about Albert having received support in this way from the USA, but the link, somewhat out on a tangent, was to bring big problems to EAB following Albert's death. Frank assured the Committee that Ralph had said that upon going to Brazil *"he would do nothing to undermine Frank's authority"*, but that was exactly what he did do. Frank also stated to the Committee that Moulton, having supported Albert Mundy in the past, *"had now agreed to support Xandu and two native workers"*. Here then was an explosive and destructive mixture, if ever there was one! Theologically Ralph and Xandu were oceans apart. Ralph was a fundamentalist Baptist, strictly non-Pentecostal, and certainly non-legalistic. Xandu was at the opposite end of the theological spectrum and in neutral circumstances they would have been the last to unite forces. However, Ralph Moulton had money and somehow felt his years of support gave him some right to take over EAB. Xandu Soares liked his money, and also felt that as she had been a dominant figure near to Albert Mundy for decades this also gave her the right to run EAB. They thus were to unite in an unholy alliance against Frank Dyer's leadership, winning over Albert's son, Graham, who was also seduced by financial possibilities ahead; and convincing him of the rights of his 'hereditary peerage' sought to use Graham as a pawn figure ahead of a coup d'état; reducing Frank Dyer's leadership to irrelevance and the EAB UK Committee to wag the tail of a dog called "Uncle Sam", albeit with a Brazilian yellow t-shirt with a big X (for Xandu) on it!

As the black storm clouds loomed not far ahead for EAB, though the thunder could not yet be heard, Frank Dyer was evaluating the situation in which EAB found itself. Frank initially wrote in the GTB News of March, 1972:

"I need your prayers continually because the responsibility is great. Nevertheless, in spite of many problems, the Lord is blessing the work. Some have asked me to give some details of our workers so here are the names of the more prominent ones.

Xandu Soares has been in the work since the time Brother and Sister Mundy were in Princesa Isabel between 1940 and 1948. She lives in Patos but travels round the field from here and is now supported by the Princess Anne Baptist Church in the USA.

This same church now supports Evangelist Miguel Serafim who works in the Malta and Condado region and was supported by GTB up to last year.

Manoel Alves Queiroz (Manoel Lourenço) works in Boqueirão and Serra Grande and was converted back in 1949 when Bert and I ministered at Serra Grande.

Edivaldo Rodrigues and Elpídio Xavier are engaged in tent campaigns and until recently both were supported by GTB, but now the former is also supported by the USA.

There is also José Domingos who is leading the work at Campina Grande, and Evangelist Zacarias Salvador who has gone to take on the work at Princesa Isabel.

At Itaporanga the leader was Cesar Juvenal, but he had to flee for his life, so we have appointed Antonio Ferreira to lead the church there.

In São Paulo the main leaders are José Henrique, at Itaím Paulista, and José Leite at Mauá.

Besides the above mentioned places we send workers most Sundays from the Patos church to Passagem, where Antônio Macena was used of the Lord to win six souls recently, and every other Sunday a truck, which belongs to Pedro Guedes, goes up the mountain to Teixeira to hold a service there.

We are encouraged too by some inroads at Água Branca where we have long preached but at last we are seeing some conversions there. The numbers continue good in Patos and in fact I think it can be said that in almost every place there is an increase".

22. New Missionaries for Brazil

On 25th March 1972 Elizabeth gave birth to our first child, Deborah, in London, and in the May 1972 GTB News it was announced that "John & Elizabeth Medcraft with baby Deborah" would be leaving for Brazil to work with EAB on 3rd August that year. Two farewell services were announced; with the first in Southampton on 29th July and the other in London two days later. Prior to leaving, Elizabeth and I travelled a lot visiting a variety of churches endeavouring to raise support for the work we were to launch into that year. It was a venture of faith as it always has been; for we had no guaranteed support from anyone, but travelled round sharing what God had put in our hearts and what we dreamed of achieving for Him in Brazil. I remember our itinerary around County Durham where we visited many churches where we had links, owing to my mother's birthplace having been at Bishop Auckland. We visited many churches in the Hampshire area and in London and Essex. As well as having the great help of Elizabeth who of course had been born, brought up, and educated in Brazil until 16 years of age, I had Portuguese lessons at the "House of Brazil" in Lancaster Gate, London. Dona Lydia was a wonderful middle aged lady from Rio de Janeiro and taught me a lot. She used an early version of the communicative approach in language teaching, with no memorization exercises which never work for me. It was such a wonderful baptism into Brazilian culture as I made friends with many Brazilians at the House who were in London doing post-graduate studies and the likes. I already knew all the Brazilian hymns Elizabeth had on records, but now I was introduced to Chico Buarque, Jair Rodrigues, Jorge Ben and other great Brazilian singers I had never heard before:

> *"Estava à toa na vida*
> *O meu amor me chamou*
> *Pra ver a banda passar*
> *Cantando coisas de amor"*
> (Chico Buarque – A Banda)

"Prepare o seu coração pras coisas que eu vou contar
Eu venho lá do sertão, eu venho lá do sertão
Eu venho lá do sertão e posso não lhe agradar
Aprendi a dizer não, ver a morte sem chorar"
(Geraldo Vandré – Disparada)

When I got to Brazil my Evangelical Christian brothers and sisters told me I couldn't like these sort of songs! I liked them anyway. The legalists started working on me from day one!

(Lt to Rt: Me, Frank, Liz, Esther, Ivy & Deborah (in arms)
arriving at Recife Airport

Our Portuguese Airlines (TAP) Boeing Jet touched down at Recife Airport at 1.45 p.m. on Thursday 3rd August 1972, and Frank, Ivy and Esther were there to meet us. It was decided to make the 270 mile journey that evening in the late Albert Mundy's 'Rural truck' and were we glad to finally reach Patos at 2 a.m. Baby Deborah settled in very well and had no early health problems which was quite a relief because Eddie Irish, of the EAB Home Committee, had been very reticent to agree to us going to Brazil with such a young baby, in the light of all that the Mundys had gone through with their family. I suffered a lot with the mosquitoes at first, but got used to them. Nowadays I can watch dozens on my legs in the evening and they have no more effect!

We were given a traditional welcome service at the EAB Patos church on Saturday 5th August. About a month later I wrote a letter, on 7th September–Brazil's 150th Independence Day– (to be read at the 34th annual celebration of EAB in Southampton. We had watched a tremendous civic celebration of this in the centre of town that morning and parts of it I still have on Super-Eight silent film. Clearly I had been impressed by the patriotic fervour. My letter arrived in time for the EAB Annual meeting on 16th September in Southampton, where Dr. Leslie Greening was the speaker and the Romsey Ambassador Choir sang.

23. Dark Clouds gather

One great problem that EAB had in this period of transition from a charismatic founder leader, Albert Mundy, to a different style of leadership under Frank Dyer, was the fact that EAB had never drawn up a Constitution or been officially legally registered. There was nothing on paper that had been previously agreed so as to say how things should carry on following the death of the EAB founder, and this created great problems. It is true that Frank Dyer had been appointed Field Superintendent by the EAB Board in the UK, but EAB was now 34 years old and the EAB Board did not have the influence on the ground in Brazil of earlier years.

Albert Mundy had always been a visionary leader with great courage and dedication as he blazed pioneer trails with the Gospel of Christ. Unfortunately he had never found the time, amidst all this, to structure the work in terms of long-term organization, and this was to be a job that would very soon fall to me. Frank Dyer expressed his feelings in the November 1972 edition of the GTB News:

Although I had been a co-worker for so many years with our late Brother Mundy, yet in Patos I have not found it easy to take his place. Some have been seeking to usurp authority almost to the point of making a division and this has been further complicated by an outside influence...The Moultons arrived from the USA on September 21ˢᵗ ".

Despite all the tension, as a result of the post-Mundy era power struggle, we endeavoured to double up our efforts ministering in a variety of places around the field, with usually Frank and me alternating who travelled and who stayed at base. It was just as well I came to Brazil with a fair basic idea of Portuguese and was able to lead services and preach within six weeks of arrival, not that the fluency was perfect, but I could get by. Thus amidst all the stress and tension we still managed to minister at Serra Grande, Aguiar, Escurinho, Genipapo, Itaporanga, São José de Caiana,

Coremas, Catingueira, Passagem, Teixeira and Cacimba de Areia. (GTB News – November 1972)

So it was that the situation on the field was tense but by no means amounted to a paralysis of the work. In fact on 15th March 1973, I had the joy of travelling with Frank and a group from Patos on Elder Pedro Guedes's truck to lay the foundation stone for a new EAB church at Ibiara, 100 miles west of Patos. This was an unusual case as the possibility of building a church arose there when a lady from Recife, whose late husband was from Ibiara originally, and had got converted in Recife, wanted us to build an evangelical church in Ibiara in his memory and to fulfill a wish he had long held.

With all the tension in the air, Frank returned the Mundys' vehicle to the family and bought himself an old 1960 jeep. I initially followed the EAB tradition of missionaries always having old vehicles falling apart, and bought an old 'Rural' truck produced by Ford Wyllis. During the few months I had it the truck caught fire three times, and was a constant liability, which made me raise with Frank the sense of EAB vehicle policy. To start with I was not a mechanical type, as was Frank, and as I saw it I hadn't come to Brazil to spend most of my time under a vehicle fixing it. With no on-the-road AA-type assistance available, and with late night journeys back from services on roads out in the wilds, we came to the agreement that it was dangerous and really irresponsible to carry on in this way; so in the 1970s Frank purchased a new 'Rural' truck and I bought a Kombi. A new approach had been taken by EAB and it meant we could get much more done for God.

Despite all the attempts to maintain normality in the Mission, things got steadily worse during 1973. It was the most tragic year in EAB history. Graham Mundy returned to Brazil *"to take the place of his father"* and he was funded by the wealthy American, Ralph Moulton, who also moved to Patos. Graham Mundy was also morally supported by Xandu Soares, who had been accustomed to run so much when Albert Mundy was alive, being his right-hand woman. My first year in the work of God in Brazil was a baptism of fire, and I could clearly observe the intransigent determination of Xandu Soares and Ralph Moulton, using Graham Mundy who was by now calling himself quite ludicrously *"Pastor Graham Mundy"*, as a pawn to flout his non-existent hereditary rights to the EAB 'throne' and depose Frank Dyer to take over the Mission lock, stock and barrel.

As I have researched all EAB historical documents available, so as to write this history, it strikes me as additionally sad that this work of treachery and disloyalty was carried out with Frank Dyer who was the last person to deserve it. Constantly, over the years, Albert Mundy has left on record his indebtedness to Frank's support and faithfulness, backing his leadership at all times. Albert refers to times when he was on furlough and attempted revolts did occur in his long periods of absence, but it was always Frank that held the fort and resisted such moves.

Things really came to a head in August 1973, exactly one year after my arrival in Brazil, and I stood firm with Frank, as I always did till the day he died. Graham Mundy sent a letter to Frank Dyer on 26th August 1973, inviting him to a special meeting in the Patos church that afternoon at 2 p.m. The letter was hand-written on EAB headed paper and I have the original. The audacity of this letter is underlined when one considers the fact that Frank Dyer had been pastor and co-pastor of that church, off and on, over 24 years, living a holy and dedicated life to God. Now here was Graham inviting him to a meeting at the church where he was the pastor! We, of course, rejoice that Graham committed his life to Christ in this very church in 2007, but sadly it is undeniable that he had never ever even been any sort of Christian worker with EAB, or any other organization, and his status then before the Lord was ill defined. Frank could see the writing on the wall so, realizing the meeting was one of rebellion, he did not go.

Two days later things got even worse when, this time typed, and signed by *"Pastor Graham Mundy"*, he wrote in registered letter number R8927 which I have in its original form:

"28th August, 1973.

Dear Mr Frank Dyer,

You were invited to a meeting on August 26th, 1973, and you did not turn up. I therefore inform you that you are dismissed from the pastorate of the church.

At the same meeting Graham Mundy was elected to be the pastor of the church, and on September 8th, 1973, he will take up office.

Pastor Graham Mundy".

Thus Frank Dyer could see before him a lifetime of service to God and EAB under total threat by totally unscrupulous behaviour, and he knew his responsibility was to act firmly and in love to save the Mission from destruction. Frank, after all, had been at the docks in 1938 to see the Mundys off to Brazil; was also a member of the first EAB Home Committee ever formed; had been an EAB Missionary since 1949; and had been EAB Field Director since 1971. Thus Frank asked me and Elizabeth to draw up an emergency constitution, in total secrecy, so as to register the Mission legally with the authorities (as ought to have been done years previously); and thus guarantee that the coup and take-over could not be accomplished. Elizabeth and I worked day and night, till very late hours, drawing up the constitution, and with Frank's approval, I rushed on a night coach to the state capital and successfully registered "Ação Evangélica". Praise the Lord! We then were immediately able to obtain a legal injunction prohibiting the proposed 8th September induction of Graham Mundy as the Pastor of the EAB church, or any other such meeting that was not authorized by the legal director, Pastor Frank Dyer.

It was an awful battle. It was horrifically stressful. Yet it was a great victory for the Gospel and the Mission, which this year celebrates 74 years existence and has yet many more ahead as Jesus enables and tarries. We would have preferred the registration of the Mission to have happened under more pleasant circumstances, and clearly we would have preferred not to have had to use a legal injunction to save EAB. However it was the lesser of two evils, the greater which would have been the destruction of years of work which had been carried out entirely for God's glory.

It took time for EAB and its newly registered indigenous national church, 'Ação Evangélica' (ACEV), to recover from such trauma. More damage was done to the Gospel in Patos by a small group of determined rebels against God's anointed one in 1973, than all the raging masses that had sought to destroy the Gospel in Patos fifteen years earlier. However God has his ways to remove obstacles, and straight after this Ralph Moulton had a similarly arrogant confrontation with a Brazilian policeman who did not react in a calm Christian manner as Frank. The policeman was so furious that he threatened to kill the American and drew his revolver. Ralph Moulton fled the country never to be seen again. Graham, sadly, went away from God altogether, but I stress how overjoyed we were to see him back to God before he died. We forgave Graham and did all we could to help in his life with God in his last years, but we cannot erase history and cannot leave out this sad chapter of EAB history so as to be transparent and honest. Yes, EAB went through all this, but God is good and gave us the victory, and today the work is bigger and stronger by far than ever before for the glory of God! At the time Xandu Soares led a group of rebels out of the church and spent many of the latter days of her life on a bed of sickness and awful suffering, but she never made her peace with us. The group she led out has splintered in many directions.

The lessons are many to be learnt from EAB's 1973. A Mission must increasingly improve its organizational structure as it grows and prepare for the future in which no one of us is eternal. There are no hereditary peerages in God's work, but God chooses and uses whom He wills, according to the gifts with which He equips His people. God's will is expressed in the unanimous consensus of His people and not according to anyone's nationality, status, wealth or family ties. Of course we love to see our children in the work of the Lord, but it always must be God who directs to each role and position in his church, as expressed by the church – the community of faith. Another lesson learnt from EAB's 1973 is that not only good things happen on the mission field as some missionaries sometimes give the impression, leaving Christians in the UK sometimes depressed. Bad things, terrible things, happen too. But God is faithful, and if we do our part in love and humility, he is able to restore the damage and years that the locusts have eaten. That is what God has and is doing for EAB, and we praise him for it.

24. A Brighter Day

On 2nd October 1973 we held a surprise thanksgiving service for Frank and Ivy Dyer's 25th wedding anniversary. The youth presented a special programme of hymns and poems, and then I preached on the *"Marriage at Cana of Galilee"*. *"Whatsoever he saith unto you, do it",* was suggested to have been the formula for 25 years happy marriage! *"Thou has kept the best wine until last",* was what we trusted would be their experience in the years ahead! Then in the Christmas play of 1973 Elizabeth was a flower and I was a shepherd!

Reports at the end of 1973and going into 1974 told of blessing on churches at Santa Terezinha; Cacimba de Aréia; Maturéia in the state of Paraíba; and at Jasmin in Pernambuco. Then too at Princesa Isabel and Tavares, but Princesa Isabel was reported as being really run down, with the few Christians there having moved away to find work –including Manoel Jorge de Oliveira who was converted in 1970 and later returned and is today the local pastor of a thriving church. Itaporanga and Conceição were reported doing well too. In February 1974 I was chosen by the united youth in Patos to be the chairman of the Evangelical Youth Association, and that month in the carnival period I took the youth to a camp at Campina Grande for the first time ever! Then too, the May 1974 edition of GTB News told of ministry at Palmeiras and Imaculada, and decisions for Christ were reported at Campina Grande.

Another positive dividend of the 1973 uprising and its eventual solution was the uprooting of the chief legalists from the Patos church, meaning that slowly we started to breathe purer air in this sphere, with less attention given to man-made extra rules and regulations. Had this not been the case, the youth would never have been allowed to go to a camp, as had now happened. A new EAB/ACEV was emerging.

The 1974 EAB/ACEV Field Conference in Patos

In the middle of 1974 however, I contracted typhoid and was very ill for a considerable period. Having recovered from this, the doctors said that I would not enjoy full health again unless I had my tonsils removed; this I stupidly agreed to have done in the Patos General Hospital by local anaesthetic. It was an awful experience, which resulted in a serious post-operation infection, and so I was again bombarded with more and more antibiotics. Thus it was that on 6th November 1974, Elizabeth, who was pregnant, two and a half year old Deborah, and I went for a furlough in the UK for me to recover from months of ill health. Surely all the stress of the recent turmoil had not helped either. It was quite something for a young green missionary to cope with. Thus Frank Dyer wrote to the EAB Committee in the UK concerning my need for a break in England:

"John, Elizabeth and Deborah are returning to rest, following John's protracted illness. The doctors here nearly killed him by prescribing so many strong antibiotics, but they all seemed to be at a loss as to how to treat his constant high temperature. The first term has been very hard on them, but they have seen fruit. Many have been blessed through their ministry and a number have made decisions for Christ. Also John was able to give me invaluable help in registering the work with the Brazilian authorities. Pray for them and us. We keenly feel the separation".

After a good rest back in the UK I was feeling much better, and was happy to take part in the 18th March 1975 UK Committee meeting, at which Eddie Irish, Stanley Dibden, Jack Dyer, Deryck Scard, Clifford Sims and Joyce Sims were present, together with Neil Parsons and my late father, George Medcraft; who had both recently been invited to join the Board. That year, Clifford Sims was to retire from his EAB role. I was asked by Frank Dyer to give a detailed first hand account of all the 1973 incidents, and their on-going repercussions, to the Committee and this I did. I also proposed to the Committee that EAB should revert to a better quality printed News Bulletin, and this was agreed to.

Sadly, four days after this meeting, our new baby, John Frank George Medcraft, whom we called Johnny, died with meningitis. It was another period of devastating sadness for us.

Nevertheless in April 1975 the new style GTB News came out with a photo and properly printed. Supporters had not seen this type of publication for years, and it did make things a lot more attractive and presentable. Frank Dyer reported in this edition that *"a steady stream of decisions were being made in Campina Grande"*. He also reported blessing at Itaporanga and Tavares; and at Cedro where there were four decisions for Christ. Frank also refers to having *"baptized two whilst there in a nearby lake"*. I wrote in the same edition about news I had received from Evangelist Antônio Manoel dos Santos at Conceição, where God was also blessing the work.

In August 1975, the next edition of the new GTB News was circulated and this even had two photos! Frank was clearly encouraged by how the work was going at Campina Grande, and he had carried out a baptism there. He was proud to say that the tent he brought out in 1949 was still being used as a changing room for baptisms by lakes and rivers! More had been baptized at Conceição, he said, and he also ministered at Cachoeirinha; Ibiara; Conceição; Itaporanga; Princesa Isabel, where another five were baptized; Tavares; Maturéia; and Teixeira; as well as at the headquarters church in Patos. The Lord was blessing, and the dark clouds were giving way to Brazilian sunshine in the work of EAB again. In this edition of the GTB News, a photo and testimony from Evangelist Zacarias Salvador Pereira were published:

"I accepted the Lord into my life on October 12th, 1946. I was always timid and scared to speak in public, and imitated a cough if I thought I was to be asked to give a word! I woke up about living more fully for God after having been healed from a serious illness and told the Lord I would work for him. Pastor Albert Mundy asked me to testify after this and I think he was almost shocked that I did just that! My wife, Regina, and I moved to Itaporanga and there the Lord helped me, and I forgot that I didn't know how to preach! I have never stopped preaching the Gospel ever since and am happiest trekking on foot over the mountain passes taking the saving message of the grace of Christ to so many who have never heard. What a thrill it is when later I call up the pastors to baptize new converts in these out in the wilds places".

By late 1975 Elizabeth, Deborah and I were busy on deputation work for EAB around a great variety of churches in the UK. The good news in the December issue of the GTB News was that the youth in Patos had held their own convention in late October; with early morning prayer, afternoon street evangelism, and evening services in the church. Two young people were baptized in the convention, and the youth came to life as a result of it. Each Saturday, from then on, they started gathering in the afternoons to practice singing, then going out to evangelize on the streets, and finally to hold an open-air service each Saturday evening. The GTB News closed by announcing our farewell service for 21st February 1976, as we prepared to return to Brazil on 8th March. The speaker was Jean-Jacques Zbinden, singing was provided by a group from the IBTI, and Deryck Scard chaired the service. Prior to this I spent part of January and February in a freezing cold Canada, at the invitation of ex-missionary Rodney Morgan who had had long term connections with my church of origin in London. I ministered in the Winnipeg and Calgary areas.

My 1976 diary reads as follows:

"March 8th: Left Heathrow at 6.30 p.m. on a KLM Trident Three for Amsterdam. Changed at Amsterdam to a Super DC8.

March 9th: Stopped at Monrovia, Liberia, West Africa at 4 a.m. (GMT) The airport was very dark and hot. We bought drinks and beads as souvenirs. We arrived at São Paulo at 10.30 a.m. having stopped on the way at Rio de Janeiro for two hours. We flew over the Statue of Christ and the famous beautiful beaches there. We were met in São Paulo by Ray and Heather Saunders who had just come to work in Brazil. We stayed with them till the 13th.

March 13th: Went to spend time ministering at the EAB churches at Mauá and Itaím Paulista in Greater São Paulo until April 4th. Whilst there we were able to purchase a Ford Wyllis Rural Truck like Frank had already. (We had sold our Kombi went we went on furlough)

April 4th: Left São Paulo for Rio de Janeiro driving the 268 miles in our new truck. We ministered at a Baptist church where Elthan, a member of the Brazilian navy that we had met in Southampton, was the pastor. We visited Copacabana and Ipanema beaches and the Statue of Christ in the days when Rio de Janeiro was a peaceful city.

April 6th: We drove 465 miles north today to visit old Peniel Chapel Missionaries, Ivy Roult and the Squair Family, at Teófilo Otoni in the state of Minas Gerais. It was lovely to have fellowship with them and to preach in the church founded by the missionary society in London where I was born and brought up.

April 12th: We finally arrived in Patos, in the north-east, having driven 1,280 miles from Teófilo Otoni, and a total distance from São Paulo of just over 2,000 miles. Looking back it was clearly the sort of adventure one would only undertake when young. For Elizabeth and me to have travelled 2,000 miles with just little Deborah, who had her 4th birthday on the journey, was at the least very risky!"

We received a very warm welcome back in Patos and we got straight into the ministry groove in Patos and Campina Grande, where Francisco Farias and his wife Eva were now leading the church. They married in an unusual way – by proxy! On 29th April 1976, we rented a house at 682, Augusto dos Anjos Street, in Patos. We also preached in Santa Terezinha, Piancó, Cacimba de Aréia, Itaporanga, Conceição, Capim, Pedra Branca, Nova Olinda, Santana dos Garrotes, Ibiara, Santana de Mangueira, Catingueira, Princesa Isabel, Olho D'Água, and Maturéia in Paraíba state that year, as well as São José do Egito and Jasmin in Pernambuco state. Many of these places were visited repeatedly.

In the latter part of 1976 I commenced a happy relationship with ABU (Aliança Bíblica Universitária), which is the Brazilian Inter-Varsity Fellowship, and for six years I worked in a support role training evangelical students to evangelize their fellow students, alongside regular EAB work. I became regional secretary for ABU in the whole of the north-east of Brazil between 1980 and 1982 and I found this an intellectually stimulating field of work. The in-depth Bible studies of ABU were a blessing to my life and my progress with the Portuguese language was enhanced greatly through constantly rubbing shoulders with university students and professors. I made many friends through ABU, like Professor Robinson Cavalcanti (today an evangelical Anglican Bishop), and I had the honour to be John Stott's chaufeur in Recife when he was the main speaker at the ABU National Conference in 1981.

Frank Dyer's report on 1976 was mixed, as is often the case in any Mission. The Conceição church was doing well as were those at Campina Grande and Princesa Isabel. In fact the consecration of a new deacon on 18th January was a landmark, and finally Princesa Isabel was re-gaining steam and growing again. The name of the new deacon, converted in 1970, was Manoel Jorge de Oliveira, and he was to eventually become the first ordained EAB pastor on 14th October 1984. This pastor continues leading the church to this day, and it has become a consolidated missionary church affecting the whole region. What a difference good leadership makes!

On the other hand, Frank Dyer reported stagnation in the work at Itaporanga and Teixeira that year. By 11th October 1976, however, Frank Dyer laid the foundation stone for a church building at Campina Grande (see below). Finally the end of rented garages and scruffy halls was in sight. That year ended on a happy family note too when our second daughter, Lynn Amanda, was born on 14th December.

25. Princesa Isabel grows again

Missionary work is all about persistence. You have got to stick at
the job and leave the rest to God. Sometimes things go well, and at
other times it is quite the opposite, but God's truth will ultimately
be victorious, if we are faithful and trust in Him.

EAB's church at Princesa Isabel is a classical example of this. To
start the church at all in the 1940s was very difficult, but the
church was planted and grew to a number around 50. Then people
moved away with the droughts and the work came apart somewhat.
Frank Dyer went there in the early 1950s but could make little
headway in the place. In fact, in the 1950s and 1960s the church
virtually came to a halt. I remember going there soon after arriving
in Brazil in 1972 with Frank Dyer. We held a service in the church
but found no Christians in the town. We found maize growing, of
all places on the roof of the church. Clearly a bird must have
planted it there and somehow the maize grew! When we opened
the front doors of the church, Frank and I were horrified as the
building was thick with bat droppings on the floor and the smell
was intense. However we got to work and shovelled out the
droppings and washed and cleaned the entire church. Some came
to hear the Gospel there that night. It was worth the effort.

After this Manoel Jorge, who had been converted there in 1970,
returned to Princesa Isabel, God used him, and things started to
pick up. Manoel Jorge had been converted during the three year's
ministry of Evangelist Zacarias in the church. In fact the only
conversion that occurred during those three years was that of
Manoel Jorge. It was the seed of the church's revival in the 1970s,
and by 1977 the GTB News was quite ecstatic about what was
happening at Princesa Isabel. For Manoel Jorge had returned from
his trip away to find work and had a new vigour and touch from
the Lord. Thus he focused on sharing the Gospel with his extended
family in the town as at least they had to listen to him, even though
it was only out of politeness to a relative. Slowly but surely God
began to break hardened hearts and people started to commit their

lives to Christ. When I went to preach there in mid 1977 I found 87 in the church! Revival indeed!

Manoel Jorge in the 1970s

Frank Dyer ministered at Princesa Isabel in November 1977 and baptized another seven new converts in the lake at Cedro in that County. However 1977 was not all positive and our children suffered a battering in their health. Baby Lynn almost died when we were visiting Conceição. She suddenly developed dysentary and a high fever threw her into convulsions. I was called out of church in the middle of a sermon to this scene, and upon rushing Lynn to the small local hospital we found the doctor drunk who pronounced her "beyond hope". Gladly one of our church members, Miriam, who was in church that night and was a nurse, came to the hospital, injected medication into Lynn's vein, got her out of the convulsion, put her on a drip which we hooked up in the car, and we sped back the 107 miles of earth track to Patos, as if we were in a Formula One race or Paris – Dakar Rally! Lynn was admitted to hospital in Patos by Dr. Pedro Firmino and she eventually recovered well, but it was a very big fright! That same year our other daughter, Deborah, was also very ill with foot and mouth disease. I have never seen anybody's mouth like it. It had a mass of sores so bad that she could not even drink water for days and was kept hydrated and fed by a drip. Eventually she pulled through by the grace of God.

The EAB UK Committee underwent further changes in the 1977-1978 period with Clifford Sims, Deryck Scard and Stanley Dibden retiring over a twelve month period. This was not because of any internal problems, but simply a natural turnover of membership, as those getting older felt they should make way for younger men. In 1978 David Shearing joined the Committee. David is the son of Pastor Winston Shearing, who was with EAB from the start till his death in 1971. David Moses from the north-east of England also joined the Committee at the time. This was a period in which the EAB home committee was working on registering the Mission as a charity. Thus not only had the work in Brazil created a Brazilian constitution in 1973, but now was the turn of the Mission to do this in the UK. Thus finally on 9th February 1979 EAB became a registered charity in the UK.

1977 ended on a tragic note in Brazil when one of our evangelists, Miguel Serafim, was killed in a road accident on Friday 30th December. He was the father of about 15 children. I remember clearly how he had been in the service in Patos on the Thursday, and Frank and I spoke to him after the service about the non roadworthy state of his old truck. The bearings on the wheels were very worn and the wheels had a visible wobble. We insisted with him that he should not return to Ibiara the next day where he was leading the work, without fixing the vehicle. However Miguel, with some bravado, refused to listen and said he would be alright. The next day his vehicle lost a wheel approaching Itaporanga on a bend and he was thrown out of the vehicle and killed.

The following morning I went with Frank to assist him in conducting the funeral and it was an unforgettable experience. First of all, as we walked carrying the coffin from Miguel's house to the cemetery, the cheap coffin, only covered by a material, was sagging in the middle with the weight of the body. The material also did nothing to shield us from the awful smell either. When we got to the cemetery, Frank led the burial service and preached and sang heartily as he showed me how to conduct such events. However Frank never lost his sense of humour at even moments like this, and in the middle of one hymn he nudged me, with a smirk on his face, and nodded to his right. Lo and behold there was a skull, with a full head of hair sitting looking at us, obviously having been dug up to make room for Brother Miguel in the poor section of the grave yard. I smirked back and we pressed on singing heartily! I learnt so much from Frank Dyer in Brazil, and after the service he had a good private chuckle with me about it all. It wasn't that he was calous about such things, but he had learnt to live with these unpleasant and untidy aspects of life in the Brazilian north-eastern interior. You either smiled through such incidents or cried and got depressed. Frank always smiled and trained me to be positive too, and do my best to smile in adversity and brush it off and get on with living.

On 14th January 1978 Frank and I took our vehicles loaded with helpers from Patos, to a village called Mãe D'água, to hold services for the first time. This village is only 24 miles south-west of Patos, but is is down such a rugged track off the main road routes that the EAB arquives (archives) at the time note *"how forgotten this village had been as a result"*. We felt considerable spiritual darkness and oppression in the place, and although some did listen to the preaching of the Gospel, we were looked upon as aliens from another planet and nobody responded to appeals for commitment to Christ and the Gospel. EAB has been plodding away now for the past 30 years or so and never has managed to really plant a church there, but we keep trying. We have had handfuls of believers at times but today there is just one Christian there.

Frank Dyer's diary has a note for 24th March 1978, that he had been ministering in a similar sort of place at Vazante, in the County of Diamante, on the old road to Conceição about 100 miles west of Patos. There too, we are still plodding away and still struggling to establish a church. In fact in our 70th year we had a special team making an intense effort there again to raise the name of Jesus high in the village.

On 21st April 1978 I led the inauguration of an EAB Christian Literature Centre in the Patos market. It was an idea that worked fairly well for a few years but never really took off. It was nice to have my sister Joy, and her daughter Louisa, with us for the event. They were visiting the work of the Mission for the first time in that year. The idea was for the Centre to function as a Christian Book Shop, so as to be an opening for the sale of Bibles, records and Christian literature to the general public. It seems to me that this is not an easy venture anywhere in the world and certainly in Patos we pressed on for some years, it being run daily by a young man called Luis Conserva; but we eventually closed it in the 1980s as it did not receive the response for which we had hoped. I am always full of ideas and initiatives and some work and some do not. I believe we should try different things, as sometimes the most unlikely ideas work out wonderfully well. I work on the basis that unless God gives me a clear red light then I have a green light and go for it.

My sister, Joy Levermore, who was with us at the time, sent me the following memories of her trip to the EAB field of service:
"We arrived Christmas 1977 and paid £100 in excess luggage! Well dad did!! Brought 2 christmas cakes, home made two puddings and loads of other things!

Heat was overpowering, I can remember getting off the plane and feeling as if I had walked into a very hot oven. I remember it was early morning, direct flight from Heathrow to Recife. I will never forget the sight of young children sleeping under the cars in the car park, I had never seen anything like it.

Louisa was 18 months old! Louisa was born in July 76 and I think Lynn Dec 76, I know they were very near in age and for some reason Louisa enjoyed biting Lynn and Liz had to make a barracade in the lounge to keep them apart.

I remember the ants, the cockroaches and a large lizard that got stuck behind the bookcase. Also the very large frogs outside the house under the street lamps and a snake on the front path one night.

I remember the poverty, the amount of people who died and the church bells that would ring out for a funeral. I remember going to the Patos church for the funeral of a church deacon and standing at the open coffin.

I remember Liz buying a tin tub of ice-cream and when we got half way through we found a cockroach in the middle and much to my dismay had to throw it all away. I remember salad being washed in Milton and all water being filtered.

I remember carrying milk from the milk lady in the boiling morning sun and buying bread every evening for tea.

I REMEMBER MOSQUITOS!!! but on that trip I do not remember them as much as the ants, you dropped a crumb and they arrived from everywhere.

I remember Pedro and Rebecca especially and trying to talk to them in Portuguese. I remember going with Pedro to the hospital and thinking I should wear tights to look smart much to everyone's amusement.

I remember trying to learn Portuguese and enjoying talking to the maid Toyinha ? spelling.

I don't remember a swimming pool unfortunately but do remember getting sun stroke when we did make it to the beach as I would'nt stay in the shade and Liz washed her hands of me!! and did I suffer. I lost all of the top layer of my skin and blacked out everytime I sat up!!

I remember losing lots of weight but unfortunately it did not last!

I remember a pet duck being killed to eat and Deborah sitting at the table and refusing to take a bite.

I remember large water melons.

I remember the carnival camp.

146

I remember travelling in the boiling heat to visit a tiny village and sleeping in a hammock with Louisa in a stone built hut. I remember accepting the offer of a shower when we arrived late at night only to be told by John that it was a jug of water at the bottom of the garden. I declined politely.

I remember washing with a jug of water at the end of the garden the next morning with just string and cardboard around me trying to desperately not to surface above chest level! When I did venture my head above the flapping cardboard there was a large group of adults and children and a donkey watching me. The 'shower' had a concrete slab which you stood on which also when moved served as a toilet!! With cockroaches running everywhere!

I remember against advice eating small fruit off a tree and getting dysentery!

I remember lovely friendly simple people who would give you all they had.

I remember singing in Portuguese in the Christmas eve service!

I remember sitting in boiling heat in church with the fans above.

I remember visiting Frank and Ivy's house.

I remember a happy time in a country so far removed from what I had been born into and knowing that you truly had to be called of God to work there"!! (Joy Levermore – written on 28th April 2008)

On 3rd July 1978, our son Philip Stephen was born in Patos. The Mission's news bulletin of that period also announced that the government was building a new tarmac road from Patos, up the mountain to Teixeira and then all the way along the montain ridge through Maturéia, Imaculada, Água Branca, Juru and Tavares as far as Princesa Isabel! It was a dream come true, as no longer would we be shaken to bits going along that unbelievably bumpy road preaching the Gospel. Now in EAB's 40th year the link between our original base at Princesa Isabel and our current base in

Patos was being streamlined by tarmac, and in the 40th anniversary service in the UK that year, James Forsythe, from Northern Ireland, was the speaker and Rodney Shearing was the soloist.

Thus I conclude the first volume of EAB history (1938 – 1978) and I hopefully will, if God permits, yet write the second 40 years of our history because EAB marches on with:-

- vastly increased national team of pastors
- expanding church planting
- increasing pioneer projects

"The end is not yet – praise the Lord!"

Cover photos

- The microphone on the front cover was taken to Brazil by Frank Dyer in 1957 together with the loudspeaker on the back cover.
- The typewriter was Albert Mundy's.
- The communion chalice was taken to Brazil in EAB's early years by Albert Mundy and used in the communion services in the Patos church. The chalice presumably was donated to EAB to this end. It is engraved with "Uppingham School Athletic Sports 1876 – Half Mile Under 15 – Second Prize – A. Drake".
- The mandolin belonged to Daisy Mundy and the violin to Graham Mundy.
- The record player belonged to Frank Dyer and worked on 16, 33, 45 and 78 rpm.
- The charcoal iron belonged to Ivy Dyer as did the sewing machine.
- The Tilly lamp was taken to Brazil by Frank Dyer in 1949 and the Gestetner printer was also taken to Brazil by Frank Dyer in 1957 to print Gospel literature.

The Author

John Philip Medcraft (MA) is a London-born naturalized Brazilian who has worked with EAB since 1972 and been co-director with his wife Elizabeth since 1987. He is the elected chairman of both ACEV (the evangelical church denomination founded by EAB) and its NGO 'ACEV Social'. John can be contacted at eabrazil@gmail.com

Another book by John:

Notting Hill to Brazil (2008)

16411041R00081

Made in the USA
Charleston, SC
19 December 2012